A FAREWELL TO ARMS

The War of the Words

TWAYNE'S MASTERWORK STUDIES

Robert Lecker, General Editor

A FAREWELL TO ARMS

The War of the Words

Robert W. Lewis

TWAYNE PUBLISHERS • New York
MAXWELL MACMILLAN CANADA • Toronto
MAXWELL MACMILLAN INTERNATIONAL • New York Oxford Singapore Sydney

Twayne's Masterwork Studies No. 84

A Farewell to Arms: The War of the Words
Robert W. Lewis

Twayne Publishers   Maxwell Macmillan Canada, Inc.
Macmillan Publishing Company   1200 Eglinton Avenue East
866 Third Avenue   Suite 200
New York, New York 10022   Don Mills, Ontario M3C 3N1

Macmillan Publishing Company is part of the Maxwell Communication Group
of Companies.

Library of Congress Cataloging-in-Publication Data

Lewis, Robert W. (Robert William), 1930–
    A farewell to arms : the war of the words / Robert W. Lewis.
      p.   cm. — (Twayne's masterwork studies ; no. 84)
    Includes bibliographical references and index.
    ISBN 0-8075-8052-1 (alk. paper) — ISBN 0-8057-8102-1 (pbk. : alk. paper)
    1. Hemingway, Ernest, 1899–1961. Farewell to arms. 2. World War.
  1914–1918—Literature and the war. I. Title. II. Series.
PS3515.E37F3558   1992
813'.52—dc20   91-34026
                                                            CIP

10 9 8 7 6 5 4 3 2 1 (hc)
10 9 8 7 6 5 4 3 2   (pb)

Printed in the United States of America

For my Iliad *and* Odyssey, *Lisa and* Nina

Contents

Ernest Hemingway as a volunteer ambulance driver in Italy, 1918
No. EH 2723 P in the John F. Kennedy Library Hemingway Collection

Note on the References and Acknowledgments

The first edition of *A Farewell to Arms* was published in 1929 by Charles Scribner's Sons. Readers interested in the circumstances of its publication should consult Michael S. Reynolds's *Hemingway's First War: The Making of "A Farewell to Arms."* The standard edition of the novel is currently available in several different printings from Scribner and Macmillan. Fortunately, the pagination in these printings of the 1957 Scribner text is the same, and the parenthetical page references throughout this study are to the standard edition. Unfortunately, as Reynolds points out, no edition follows Ernest Hemingway's intentions and desires in every detail, and the deletions or changes of vulgar and erotic language, certainly realistic then and considerably less objectionable today, were made by editors against his wishes. Students interested in the original typescript of the novel can read it in the Hemingway Collection in the John F. Kennedy Library in Boston.

The Selected Bibliography lists the most relevant critical and scholarly works that have helped inform this study, but in a larger sense the study is built on years of teaching and discussing this novel with many students and colleagues who just as surely as the published scholars and critics have helped enrich my understanding and appreciation of a fine novel, the art of which increases on every reading, every encounter. Beyond works of art themselves is the great dialogue we may enter into when we read and listen to one another, and I gratefully acknowledge having shared in it with an ever-increasing and increasingly impressive group of writers, colleagues, and students.

I especially want to thank Fern Kory, who read and commented on some parts, and Max Westbrook, who read and commented on a penultimate version; the present version, however it may be flawed, is much improved because of his keen critical judgment. I also thank Ursula Hovet, who not only types but thinks and often made helpful comments or raised useful questions.

I arrived at my subtitle and section title, "The War of the Words," independently of Sandra Gilbert and Susan Gubar who subsequently used it as the subtitle of their *No Man's Land: The Place of the Woman Writer in the Twentieth Century*, Volume I, *The War of the Words* published by Yale University Press. The phrase is sufficiently good and apt, I trust, for both books.

Chronology: Ernest Hemingway's Life and Works

1899–1916 Ernest Miller Hemingway is born 21 July in Oak Park, Illinois, then a middle-class suburb of Chicago noted for its high moral tone. His father is a proud, religious medical doctor and sportsman; his mother, a gifted singer and dedicated suffragette who late in life becomes a successful painter. Hemingway attends Oak Park High School, where he is active in sports and writes for the school newspaper and literary magazine, which publishes his first short stories. The family of two boys and four girls spends its summers on Walloon Lake in northern Michigan.

1917 Graduates from high school and becomes a cub reporter for the Kansas City *Star*.

1918 Joins the Red Cross and serves with an ambulance unit in Italy. Is severely wounded by a mortar shell 8 July and spends the rest of the year in a Red Cross hospital in Milan, Italy, where he falls in love with one of his nurses, Agnes von Kurowsky.

1919 Returns to Oak Park and continues writing short stories there and in northern Michigan.

1920 Takes a job in Toronto and writes free-lance for the Toronto *Star*, returning to Walloon Lake for the summer; there his parents throw him out for insolence and idleness. In October moves to Chicago, where he meets Carl Sandburg, Sherwood Anderson, and his future wife, Hadley Richardson of St. Louis. In December begins writing for and editing the magazine *Cooperative Commonwealth* and does so until its demise in October 1921.

1921 Marries Hadley Richardson on 3 September and takes a part-time job with the Toronto *Star* to write feature stories in Europe. In December he and Hadley sail for Paris.

1922	In Paris meets Ezra Pound, Gertrude Stein, James Joyce, and William Bird, newsman and publisher. As roving correspondent for the Toronto *Star,* Hemingway covers the Genoa Conference on International Economics, the Greco-Turkish War, and the Lausanne Peace Conference. In December Hadley loses his suitcase containing nearly all his literary manuscripts.
1923	He and Hadley vacation in Switzerland and visit Ezra Pound in Rapallo, Italy. Makes his first trip to Spain and in July returns to Pamplona with Hadley for his first San Fermin festival. Covers the Ruhr troubles for the Toronto *Star.* Contributes "My Old Man" to *Best Short Stories of 1923.* Robert McAlmon's Contact Editions publishes *Three Stories and Ten Poems.* Returns with Hadley to Toronto in August for the birth of their first child, John. Then resigns from the *Star* to return to Paris.
1924	In Paris becomes associate editor of Ford Maddox Ford's *Transatlantic Review.* Three Mountains Press edition of *in our time* is published in Paris.
1925	The Hemingways meet F. Scott Fitzgerald, Archibald MacLeish, Sara and Gerald Murphy, Pauline Pfeiffer, Kitty Cannell, Harold Loeb, Pat Guthrie, and Duff Twysden. Boni and Liveright publish *In Our Time.* Another trip to the Pamplona festival—with Hadley, Bill Smith, Loeb, Guthrie, and Twysden—gives Hemingway the basis for beginning *The Sun Also Rises.* Writes *The Torrents of Spring,* a satire on Sherwood Anderson. The Hemingways spend Christmas in Schruns, Austria, skiing.
1926	Liveright turns down *Torrents,* enabling Hemingway to sign a new contract with Scribner, which then publishes both *The Torrents of Spring* and *The Sun Also Rises.* Hadley and Ernest separate in August, and in November she authorizes him to start the divorce that will enable him to marry Pauline Pfeiffer.
1927	Marries Pauline Pfeiffer on 10 May in Paris. *Men without Women,* a collection of short stories, is published.
1928	Begins writing *A Farewell to Arms* and leaves Paris for Key West, Florida. Second son, Patrick, born by cesarean section in Kansas City, Missouri. Clarence E. Hemingway, Ernest's father, commits suicide 6 December because of health and financial problems.
1929	Returns with Pauline to Paris. *A Farewell to Arms* is published in September.
1930	Returns to Key West with Pauline and later visits Wyoming, where he breaks his arm in a car accident.

Chronology: Ernest Hemingway's Life and Works

1931   Third son, Gregory, born in November by cesarean section; Pauline is advised not to become pregnant again.

1932   *Death in the Afternoon* is published in September.

1933   Makes his second extended visit to Cuba and publishes a third collection of short stories, *Winner Take Nothing*. He and Pauline visit Paris on their way to a long safari in British East Africa.

1934   On return from the safari, purchases the fishing boat *Pilar* and starts a nonfiction book on hunting in East Africa.

1935   *Green Hills of Africa* is published in October.

1936   Publishes "The Short Happy Life of Francis Macomber" and "The Snows of Kilimanjaro." Meets Martha Gellhorn, like him a journalist and fiction writer, and becomes infatuated. The Spanish Civil War begins; Hemingway contributes money to provide two ambulances and agrees to cover the war for the North American Newspaper Alliance.

1937   Travels to Spain in late March and assists in the filming of a Loyalist propaganda film, *The Spanish Earth*. Begins an affair with Martha Gellhorn. *To Have and Have Not*, his fourth novel, is published in October.

1938   Returns to Key West in January but is back in Spain with Martha in March. Publishes *The Fifth Column and the First Forty-nine Stories*, his first and only play and most of the short stories published to this time.

1939   Moves to Cuba with Martha Gellhorn and begins writing his novel on the Spanish Civil War.

1940   Publishes *For Whom the Bell Tolls* and divorces Pauline. Marries Martha Gellhorn on 21 November and purchases the Finca Vigía (Lookout Farm) in Cuba for their home.

1941   He and Martha take a six-month trip to China. The Pulitzer Prize fiction committee unanimously chooses *For Whom the Bell Tolls*, but the president of Columbia University vetoes its selection; no prize for fiction is given that year.

1942   Edits *Men at War*, a collection of fiction and nonfiction. Runs an intelligence service in Cuba approved by the U.S. embassy to uncover German agents and to hunt German U-boats from his fishing boat. (He and his crew never encounter any.)

1943   Martha leaves Cuba to cover the war in Europe, and this estrangement further undermines the marriage.

1944   In May both he and Martha return to Europe as war correspondents. In late May meets and becomes infatuated with Mary

Welsh, also a war correspondent. Suffers a severe concussion in a London car crash. From July to January 1945 is a war correspondent attached to the U.S. Fourth Infantry Division in France, Belgium, and Germany.

1945   Returns to Cuba and soon Mary Welsh moves into the Finca Vigía; she obtains a divorce from her husband, and Martha Gellhorn divorces Hemingway.

1946   Marries Mary Welsh, his fourth and final wife, on 14 March. Although they travel much, their primary home remains Cuba.

1947   Works on *The Garden of Eden,* a version of which is published posthumously in 1986.

1948   Takes Mary to his favorite places in Italy and becomes enamored of the Italian Adriana Ivancich, only 19.

1949   Returns to Cuba in the spring and works on *Across the River and into the Trees,* a novel set in Italy.

1950   Spends the first three months of the year primarily in Venice and then returns to Cuba. Publishes *Across the River and into the Trees* and writes the first draft of *Islands in the Stream,* published posthumously in 1970.

1951   Starts and finishes *The Old Man and the Sea.* His mother, Grace Hall Hemingway, dies in June; Pauline Pfeiffer Hemingway dies in October.

1952   Publishes *The Old Man and the Sea,* first in a special issue of *Life* magazine and then in book form.

1953   Wins the Pulitzer Prize in fiction and spends the summer in Spain, following the bullfights. In August he and Mary travel to Kenya for his second African safari.

1954   The safari ends with two plane crashes in 24 hours, and Hemingway is reported dead. Suffering from a severe concussion, serious burns, and internal injuries, he returns to Venice in March and to Cuba in July. In October receives the Nobel Prize in literature.

1955   Starts a new African book and participates in the filming of *The Old Man and the Sea.*

1956   Spends the fall in Spain, following the bullfights, and November—January in Paris.

1957   Returns to Cuba depressed and helps in the effort to have Ezra Pound released from St. Elizabeth's mental hospital and treason charges dropped. Begins *A Moveable Feast* (1964), a book of memoirs from the 1920s in Paris.

Chronology: Ernest Hemingway's Life and Works

1958   Rents a house in Ketchum, Idaho. While there, dictator Fulgen-
            cio Batista falls, and Fidel Castro takes over the Cuban govern-
            ment.

1959   Buys a home in Ketchum. From May through October he and
            Mary follow the Antonio Ordoñez and Luis Dominguín bull-
            fights in Spain. In late fall they return to the United States,
            where Hemingway hunts and rests in Idaho.

1960   After seven months in Cuba, returns to Spain, where he suffers
            serious bouts of paranoia and depression. In November enters
            the Mayo Clinic for electroshock treatments. *Life* magazine
            publishes part of the bullfight book as "The Dangerous Sum-
            mer." (It is published in book form in 1985.)

1961   By April his depression is suicidal, and he is hospitalized twice
            in Ketchum and readmitted to the Mayo Clinic 25 April. Re-
            turns to Ketchum 30 June and commits suicide with a favorite
            shotgun the morning of 2 July.

A FAREWELL TO ARMS

The War of the Words

LITERARY AND HISTORICAL CONTEXT

1.

A World in Transition

The generation of Americans and Europeans born at the turn of the century, as Ernest Hemingway was, came of age in a turbulent era. In addition to the usual challenges of growth in which one searches for identity and selfhood in the context of family, education, and community, that generation came to maturity at the same time Europe and later the United States entered that incredibly destructive and bloody war. The Great War, like all wars, was the result of the failures of nations to resolve their differences by peaceful means. But beyond that common human defect, the Great War had dimensions of stupidity and brutality that, once apparent to its participants, made it seem the incontrovertible proof of a world without hope or reason.

The context of this war was considerably different from that of World War II. The long reign of Queen Victoria (1837–1901) had given the English language a new word, *Victorian*, not only to identify those years as a chronological period but also to name the conservatism, relative international stability, and high moral tone of the era that often masked stuffiness, banality, and the moral hypocrisy of the same age in which colonialism, child labor, and rigid class and sex restrictions were seldom questioned, let alone reformed. Europe—and to a lesser degree America—were ripe for violent and sweeping changes even while the surface of life appeared stable and calm.

Incredibly, most of the nations of Europe as well as its colonies around the world were drawn into a war that none of them had anticipated. But most of them reacted predictably to the immediate cause, the assassination of Archduke Francis Ferdinand, heir to the Austro-Hungarian throne, by a Serbian nationalist. Complicated alliances and treaties, desires for and threats to power (military and economic), real and imagined past hurts, ethnic jealousies and prides—all stirred the cauldron of war. Perhaps no one could have predicted how the immediate cause, the assassination in June 1914, could lead to a war ultimately involving more than 30 nations and 90 percent of the world's population. But inexorably, step by step, the roles were cast and the tragedy enacted. At the end, by the armistice on the Western front on 11 November 1918, 10 million had been killed and 22 million wounded, at a cost of $350 billion. Additionally, as if nature itself conspired to destroy humankind, an influenza epidemic spread around the world in 1918 and claimed almost 22 million more lives.

Factors that made World War I particularly odious were in a sense some of the same ones that had ushered in the twentieth century with prospects of growth and happiness, particularly for the very nations responsible for the bloodletting. The nineteenth century had witnessed the Industrial Revolution in which scientific discoveries and inventions were applied to the change and apparent progress of the Western nations. In the nineteenth century railroads, steel mills, oil refineries, and factories of all kinds transformed the modern world. The United States, for instance, had been primarily rural and agricultural. At the beginning of the nineteenth century, the United States was a minor nation of former colonies along the Atlantic Coast. It was a relatively prosperous country with considerable geographic advantage and economic potential but even by midcentury it was culturally underdeveloped compared with Europe. By the end of the century, it not only stretched to the Pacific but also had an empire of Caribbean and Asian colonies, an aggressive industrial and commercial upper class, a sense of "manifest destiny" that it was privileged among the nations of the earth, that it had "conquered" a continent—in short, the United States was brash and successful by the standards of the time. Of course, it also had problems—like periodic depressions; racial, regional, and religious tensions; and growing social and economic divisions—but it faced the twentieth century with optimism and great potential. Its skeptics and critics were often articulate but seldom widely heard. The adventurism of men like Theodore Roosevelt, whether on the western plains or in the White House, was more in the dominant spirit of the country than what seemed the wails of crabby old men like Mark Twain and Henry Adams in their admonitory writings.

When the Great War began in this era of transition, such old-fashioned military tactics as cavalry charges met the modern world and its technology. What died were not simply the millions scythed down by machine-gun bullets and high explosives but also many of the ideals that had brought the world's leading nations to the great debacle. Such concepts as the chivalric code of battle died too, but not easily. The Machine Age that it was hoped would make life easier and more productive also ushered in the machine gun; advanced, highly destructive artillery; barbed wire; the airplane; the submarine; poison gas; and the tank—all first used extensively in World War I. The concept of the tank derived from its benign birth in American Caterpillar tractors for agricultural and engineering use. Covered with armor plate and studded with cannon and machine guns, it became the Jekyll-Hyde instrument of doom for the lightly armed, old-fashioned individual soldier, now also vulnerable from the air and sea as well. Little wonder that the bloodied French army, led by generals adhering to outmoded tactics, revolted or that the literature of the war written by those who were in the trenches describes a world gone mad, a world in which sudden death could be a relief from mental and physical anguish.

Young men and women had, then, by and large educations and beliefs grounded in a far different world from that of the first two decades of the twentieth century. Reviewing this era in *The Modern Temper* (1929), the critic Joseph Wood Krutch grimly concluded that the old optimistic values of the nineteenth century—of a belief in human progress, the perfectibility of humankind, the inevitable success of capitalism and democracy—had perished first on the dreadful battle-fields of war and then in the halls of state in both Europe and the United States when the nations of the world could not justly and wisely restore order.

President Woodrow Wilson had campaigned for a second term and, partly on the basis that he had "kept us out of war," was reelected in 1916. One month after his inauguration he delivered his "war message" to Congress and led the United States into war against the Central Powers of Germany, Austria-Hungary, Bulgaria, and Turkey, in part because of German U-boat attacks on U.S. shipping and in part because of widely held sympathies with Britain and France. Moreover, some who opposed war felt we entered it because the overseas financial interests of capitalists like banker J. P. Morgan were in jeopardy. President Wilson's leadership was excellent, and his war aims and peace plans were idealistic, including the oft-quoted intention of "making the world safe for democracy" and his 14-point plan for postwar peace. Among Wilson's heralded points were an open peace treaty with no secret agreements, freedom of the seas, an end to discriminatory international trade practices, arms reduction, creation of new nations to give independence to nationalities formerly contained within other nations or empires, and the League of Nations.

But before his goals could be realized, other forces were already at work to ensure the failure of these and additional ideals. Although czarist Russia had been a war ally of the United States, Britain, France, and Italy, it was a repressive, totalitarian state that collapsed even before the war's end in the revolution of 1917, which eventually brought Lenin and the Bolsheviks to power. Diplomatic fighting also went on among the allies, and the defeated Central Powers suffered from the vengeance of the victors that brought them to their economic knees. The U.S. Senate refused to ratify the treaty or join the League of Nations, and as the United States turned its back on a broken, demoralized Europe that gave rise to fascism in Germany, Italy, and Spain, it entered a notorious era sometimes called the Roaring Twenties or the Jazz Age. When one considers that most of the country was not "roaring" and many citizens thought jazz music vulgar and associated with disreputable persons and activities, those epithets are shown to be somewhat misleading. In 1919, after all, the Prohibition amendment to the Constitution had been ratified, fundamental religion flourished through the decade, conservative politics dominated the country, and persons or movements thought to be radical were often suppressed; for instance, the Socialist candidate for president, Eugene Debs, was in prison when he received nearly a million votes in 1920, and organized labor suffered many setbacks in the decade, including sometimes-violent suppression of strikes.

Yet beneath the surface of daily life, other forces were at work more profoundly changing life than the headline events, and three forces could be traced to three nineteenth-century figures who triggered revolutions as sweeping in their own fields as revolutions led by a George Washington or a Lenin. The ideas of the naturalist Charles Darwin had slowly but inexorably swept aside centuries of ignorance concerning the origin of life-forms, including humanity. The tangential effect of his new theory and discoveries was to undermine fundamental religious beliefs based on the literal reading of Genesis. Humanity, Darwin understood, was subject to the same evolutionary laws as the other forms of life.

A second revolutionary whose thought would change the twentieth century was Karl Marx. Like Darwin, he was resisted not simply for his theories, the central one of which was economic determinism. That theory means that the production, distribution, and consumption of commodities were at the core of social and political systems. In capitalism, the systems resulted in an unequal and, to Marx and other egalitarians, unfair distribution of wealth. For democracies like the United States (where "all men are created equal"), the inequalities of capitalism were evident, but it was in the tyrannical czarist Russia that Marxism first began to effect the revolutionary changes that Marx and his followers sought.

Yet a third influential and revolutionary figure was to change radically our perceptions of humankind and its limitations, not to biological or economic forces beyond our individual control but to our own psychic fate. Sigmund Freud founded psychoanalysis and revealed dark aspects of human nature. Even though many of his theories have since been modified or rejected, he still remains in our cultural history the bold, imaginative explorer of our subconscious and unconscious minds and especially of our sexuality. Words like *obsession, transference, repression, the Oedipus and Electra complexes, trauma, psychosomatic, infantilism, phobia,* and *anxiety* have entered our language and thinking because of Freud, and largely in unsettling ways.

Thus, the old values of state, church, and family that writers of Ernest Hemingway's generation were born into and raised amid were mightily shaken and for some destroyed by historical circumstances (World War I chief among them) and intellectual history as well. Darwin's, Marx's, and Freud's pens could be mightier than the swords of war in changing the way we saw life and ourselves and coped with the great subjects of literature, for if the world seemed vastly changed, literature (and the other arts) still provided the means to *order* chaotic life, to give shape to complex reality. As if in compensation for or response to unusual need, Hemingway was part of a generation that grew up with the new order and similarly brought unusual talent, energy, and imagination to react to and also shape the era. While the new technology could give us Model T Fords (1905) and Thorstein Veblen's *The Theory of the Leisure Class* (1899—the year of Hemingway's birth), it was the new art that gave us the means of describing and understanding the new era.

The "modernist" movement in art from which Hemingway sprang and in which he became an acknowledged master had already been well advanced by a slightly older generation of writers. Among the Americans of this international movement were T. S. Eliot, Wallace Stevens, and Ezra Pound (poets and critics); Sherwood Anderson, Theodore Dreiser, Sinclair Lewis, and Gertrude Stein (fiction writers whose subjects and styles were refreshingly new); and the playwright Eugene O'Neill. All in various ways were to "make it new," as Pound had admonished; all were to break away from the Victorian literature of convention and propriety. Three of this group—Ezra Pound, Sherwood Anderson, and Gertrude Stein—were personally to help the young Hemingway begin his writing career after the Great War.

Whether in Paris where Hemingway moved or back in the United States, a younger generation born between 1895 and 1905 became the first full generation to inherit modernism and to come of age at the time of the war and its revolutionary aftermath. Even a partial list of them includes writers who are still widely read and admired. The earlier generation included three Nobel Prize winners—Eliot, Lewis, and O'Neill. Hemingway's generation numbered F. Scott Fitzgerald, Willa Cather, Thomas Wolfe, Hart Crane, Marianne Moore, John Dos Pasos, Edmund Wilson, William Faulkner, Langston Hughes, and John Steinbeck, among others, and it too produced three Nobel laureates in literature: Faulkner, Steinbeck, and Hemingway himself.

In a cultural sense, this use of *modern* to refer to these writers does not have a simple chronological meaning. Many of the writers and other artists contemporary to these "modernists" still followed old styles and conventions. *Modern* here refers to characteristics many if not all of which were shared by this loosely similar group of artists. It suggests "a strong and conscious break with traditional forms and techniques of expression," including a belief that in a profound way "we create the world in the act of perceiving it."[1] If so much of the world, the once-thought-stable world of certainties, was irrevocably blown away by historical and intellectual changes, why could one not heroically re-create a world for oneself through art?

Modern was thus also associated with themes of alienation, loss, and despair as its writers saw through the emptiness and hypocrisy of old ways of thinking. W. B. Yeats's Irish airman foreseeing his death in combat does so disillusioned of the "old lies":

> Those that I fight I do not hate
> Those that I guard I do not love . . .
> Nor law, nor duty bade me fight,
> Nor public men, nor cheering crowds,
> A lonely impulse of delight
> Drove to this tumult in the clouds.

In a meaningless world, a "lonely impulse" is sufficient reason to act fatalistically, even when one knows that an impulse, an instinctive or "gut" reaction, is outside the world of reason entirely. The point is, of course, that reasons, the rational, and ordered thought are all illusory, for the "modern" elevates the unconscious over the self-conscious, and here particularly the new psychology and mythology of Freud and C. G. Jung pertain. As the existentialists were to say, "Existence precedes essence." Although human beings endlessly attempt to give order and meaning to life, life itself seems to have a meaningless will of its own. Only the heroic individual confronting the absurd by making existential choices, trying to create an authentic life, can hope to find some measure of hard-won, *personal* meaning in a world of fear, alienation, despair, and madness. This was the world in which Hemingway grew up and about which he wrote in *A Farewell to Arms*.

2.

The Importance of the Work

Ernest Hemingway was a moderately prolific writer much admired by both fellow writers and an extraordinarily large reading public. The consensus among his readers and critics is that many of his short stories and at least two of his novels are his masterworks. *The Sun Also Rises* (1926) and *A Farewell to Arms* (1929) have, from their initial publication, been accorded high praise and continue to elicit admiration worldwide. The later works *For Whom the Bell Tolls* (1940) and *The Old Man and the Sea* (1952) vie with the early works for other honors, and perhaps for different reasons, but clearly *A Farewell to Arms* has entered the canon of modern literature as one of its masterpieces.

Popularity by itself, especially when sustained for more than 60 years, may provide reason enough for recognizing the importance of a work, and *A Farewell to Arms* endures because it continues to speak of the human condition to generation after generation. What is it like to be adrift, to live with uncertain personal values in a world of conflicting values? How may one discover the differences between what seems to be good, honest, true, and desirable and what actually does reward one's search and struggle? In a basic sense, *A Farewell to Arms* is a novel first of all about the education of its protagonist, Frederic Henry, and we readers vicariously live his life and learn from his hard lessons how to live. All of education (apart from what often passes as education but is really training) may be a continual search for the answer to the endlessly fascinating Socratic question "Who am I?" for it is only when one has a sense of one's authentic nature and selfhood that one may begin to know how to live. Hemingway himself was conscious of this "educational" core of the story, and four of his list of possible titles (see Oldsey) contained the very word *education* before he settled on the meaningfully ambiguous *A Farewell to Arms*.

When we read the novel carefully, we can see how it fulfills one of the ancient purposes of literature, to cast light on the world, to inform us of the human condition, to be in some way (usually indirectly) *useful*. To know is to have power, and even when the knowledge is of failure and loss, even when the story ends tragically, we have been empowered, for the story that takes us through scenes of public and private loss (the war and the death of the heroine) also confirms humanity's potential nobility. To understand (the novel in effect reveals), we must first suffer; we must go through the ancient mythical cycle of birth, death, and rebirth. Although the events and characters of the novel are original, its power comes through our recognition of how it so vividly retells the mythic story in new terms. When rites of passage such as baptism, graduation, marriage, birthdays, and funerals are embued with symbolic meaning, when they are understood as answering our need for order and recognition, then they may move and inspire us, satisfy us deeply, and help us feelingly understand, not just with our conscious minds but with our whole being. This felt-thought of metaphysical literature is at the heart of our response to *A Farewell to Arms*, and thus the measure of its greatness does lie in its enduring popularity. Its fame is not the easy success of a best-seller that fulfills a passing vogue. It endures because its story of love and war, the old combination of subjects present in literature from the time of Homer's *Iliad* and *Odyssey* to today, touches us and helps us understand the human condition.

Yet in Hemingway's novel the romantic and popular subjects of love and war are more than the positive-negative opposites of so many other stories. Finally, we are drawn to *A Farewell to Arms* not for *what* it says but for *how* it says it. If one basic purpose of literature is to instruct, the other basic purpose of literature is to *delight,* to give us pleasure in the beauty of the telling. Thus it is that this novel is recognized not solely for its tale of love and war but for the manner of its writing. If we experience a profound, cathartic feeling in the reading of this tragic story, that feeling comes not only from its mythic relevance to our humanity but also from the high artistic skill of the writing. A novel written this way about ham and eggs rather than love and war would not have greatness; there must be in all great art a blending of subject and form. In the Nobel Prize citation, this aspect of Hemingway's writing was emphasized: he received the award for his "powerful, style-making mastery of the art of modern narration."[2]

And the art of *A Farewell to Arms* is masterful. From the first descriptive sentences to the final scene on which Hemingway labored so carefully that more than 30 variants of it can be traced in the manuscript versions, the novel reads smoothly and gracefully, the greatness of its art being revealed in part because it does not draw attention to its subtle designs. Only on conscious reflection do we discover how the artist has worked his material (the words and phrases) into his design (the overall form of the plot and its subsections) to create the affects and expressions, the powerful feelings (evoked through the characterization and description), to bring us to the themes and ideas, the social dimension that fulfills our desire to find the ultimate artistic satisfaction of the blending of the true and the beautiful.

Each art is distinguished from the other arts by its medium, and the materials of literature are words. At the heart of the greatness of *A Farewell to Arms* is the artistic skill with which Hemingway uses the language. Hemingway has created not simply a story but a voice that attracts us in the very first chapter, in which the as-yet-unknown narrator describes his view of the setting, fills us with a sense of impending fate, and concludes with a mirthless irony foreshadowing other yet-unknown tragedies. In a sense, it is language itself that in the central passage of chapter 27, at a turning point in the novel, is indicted for wielding a strange power over human life. (See especially the paragraph beginning on the bottom of page 184.) Human beings are, after all, both peculiarly empowered by their unique language skills and controlled and limited by those skills. In the novel Hemingway in various artful ways keeps our attention focused on the story of love and war while at the same time he introduces the secret subject of language that parallels the one on the surface, running like a subterranean stream beneath a dry watercourse. Finally, our discovery of the ways in which Hemingway makes language itself both a subject and the medium for the story enlarges our understanding of and admiration for *A Farewell to Arms,* a novel that assured for its author an enduring eminence among the pantheon of great modern writers.

The novel and its author are also important because of their influence on other authors, other works. Many critics have applauded Hemingway's achievements and at the same time suggested the futility of imitating his original genius. Yet many have tried, picking up on one or more of his stylistic features to use in their own work. The so-called hard-boiled literature, often about detectives and criminals and characterized by clipped, laconic dialogue and understated scenes of violence, was one result of widespread admiration of Hemingway's style. Adventure narratives of all kinds in which heroic males, often with pliant, romanticized heroines, face dramatic adversities were inspired by some of Hemingway's short stories and *A Farewell to Arms*. If no one seemed to be the equal of Hemingway himself in the best of his writing, and if many misread or failed to completely perceive wherein his genius lay, nonetheless works like *A Farewell to Arms* continue to influence writers who hope to achieve some degree of his mastery of style. Like only a few other modern writers, Hemingway had made the writing of prose fiction as high an art as poetry, each phrase and sentence to be crafted carefully and imbued with both serious meaning and the transcendent delight that comes with the recognitions of art. His artistic powers are at their highest in *A Farewell to Arms*.

3.

Critical Reception

A curious coincidence marked the publication of *A Farewell to Arms* in 1929. Another novel about World War I, Erich Maria Remarque's *All Quiet on the Western Front,* was also published that year, but it describes the war from the point of view of a soldier on the other, the German, side. It was translated into English, was an immediate success, and was eventually made into a popular motion picture. Hemingway's novel was published later in 1929, and as Remarque's novel was attracting so much attention, Hemingway was concerned about how the two novels would be compared. As it turned out, his novel also became a best-seller and was made into a movie starring Gary Cooper (who later became his friend) and Helen Hayes, two of Hollywood's leading stars.

Both novelists had participated in the Great War, and both had waited 10 years before sorting out and articulating their experiences. Hemingway's first two novels, the short satire *The Torrents of Spring* (1926) and *The Sun Also Rises* (also 1926), were written quickly and soon after the events that had inspired them. The fine novel *The Sun Also Rises* stemmed from Hemingway's life in Paris in the 1920s and his holidays in Spain, where he became a serious student of the bullfights. But even though the personal and public events that formed the material for *A Farewell to Arms* had occurred by 1918, Hemingway had written only four short stories and several sketches that drew on his wartime experiences (published in his first two collections of short stories, *In Our Time* [1925] and *Men without Women* [1927]).

In March 1928, however, he began writing what he "thought was only a story," as he wrote from Paris in a letter to his editor, Maxwell Perkins. But in two weeks' time, the writing on it continued "wonderfully," and he "suddenly [got] a great kick out of the war and all the things and places and it has been going very well."[3] It had become the first draft of *A Farewell to Arms*. A month later, he was in Key West, Florida, with his second wife, Pauline. He found that remote fishing village (population then only around 10,000) a congenial place to work as well as to indulge his lifelong passion for fishing. In another letter to his editor, he again reported that the writing on the new novel was "going very well" but that when it was finished he wanted to "put it away for a couple or three months and then re-write it. The re-writing doesn't take more than six weeks or two months once it is done. But it is pretty important for me to let it cool off well before re-writing" (*Selected Letters*, 276–77). This description of Hemingway's writing habits is sound advice for any writer, and it was essential for him to follow it in order to produce the tightly controlled, well-crafted writing of the finished novel.

Hemingway continued writing the novel in Piggott, Arkansas, his wife's family home, that summer. Her first pregnancy was difficult, and the baby was delivered by cesarean section. "Pauline had a very bad time . . . and a rocky time afterwards," he wrote Perkins. "I was worried enough. Am now on page 486 . . . am going out to Wyoming. . . . Will finish the book there" (*Selected Letters*, 280). This juxtaposition of news of the difficult birth with news of progress on the novel is at once ironic and an indication of how that birth is reflected in the novel, set in far-off Europe 10 years earlier, for the heroine, Catherine, dies in childbirth. The vivid rendering of that imagined scene had a painfully close counterpart in Hemingway's life at the time he was writing the novel.

Ernest Hemingway with his father, Dr. Clarence Edmonds Hemingway, in Key West, Florida, 1928, during the writing of *A Farewell to Arms* No. *EH 8163 in the John F. Kennedy Library Hemingway Collection*

In Wyoming later that summer he wrote a letter with an amusing juxtaposition, this time a record of how many pages he had written on the novel and how many trout he had caught: "1st day—worked four pages, fished with Bill Horne caught 12. 2nd day—worked $4\frac{1}{2}$ pages, fished with two girls caught 2. 3rd day—worked zero, fished by self alone, caught 30—limit" (*Selected Letters*, 282). Nearing completion of the first draft, he seemed to have some doubts about the quality of the novel; he thought he'd rather be in Spain following the bullfights, "instead of here trying to write. To hell with novels." But a few days later he read through all he had written, almost 600 manuscript pages, and saw that it was "cockeyed wonderful" (*Selected Letters*, 283). By the end of August 1928, he had finished the first draft and was looking forward to rewriting the novel. He cautiously wrote his editor, "I believe maybe the book is pretty good [and I] have never felt better or stronger or healthier in the head or body—nor had better confidence or morale" (*Selected Letters*, 286). He had just written perhaps his best book, he was at the height of his powers, and his feelings were those of a rare peak experience.

By June 1929 Hemingway had received the galley proof of the novel and was engaged in a friendly dispute with Max Perkins over an aspect of the novel that would affect its critical reception. Hemingway was a writer of realistic fiction. One of his goals was to present stories based on life "the way it was" and not to romanticize or gloss over the rougher aspects of life. Since the subject matter included army life and a long hospital section, Hemingway often used vulgar but realistic language that by latter-day standards would be commonplace. But even after Hemingway reluctantly submitted to his editor's advice to prune or conceal with blanks possibly offensive language, some readers criticized the novel for its frankness. The old genteel tradition against which Hemingway and others of his generation were rebelling would not relent. The serialized version in *Scribner's Magazine* (which was edited even more severely than the book version that would follow) was banned in Boston by the superintendent of police. A hoped-for sale to the Literary Guild or the Book-of-the-Month Club was abandoned, and the publisher and author rode out the storm of controversy, ultimately compromising by deleting or changing then-unprintable words like *balls* (for *testicles*), *fuck,* and *shit.*

The tempest was, however, in a teapot in light of the reviews and sales that followed publication of the book version in September 1929. Two reviewers wrote negatively about the novel, although one, Harry Hansen of the New York *World,* later reversed his opinion, possibly because of the overwhelming flood of positive reviews. But another reviewer and fellow novelist, Robert Herrick, writing in the influential *Bookman,* expressed the opinions of a significant audience at the end of the decade sometimes labeled the Roaring Twenties. In fact, there were many in the nation who reacted against realistic fiction that dealt with the often-bitter truths of modern life. Herrick's review was titled "What Is Dirt?" The answer, in his puritanical view, was *A Farewell to Arms.* Even though the novel had been edited to meet Scribner's standards, the nation was divided in its tastes, and many readers still preferred not to be reminded of the "unpleasant garbage" of life (one of Herrick's phrases). To treat war and sex frankly was to run the risk of offending many readers. Herrick loftily admitted that he had read only half the novel, but that was enough for him to reach his conclusion.

Similarly, other readers of even the more severely edited magazine version wrote to Scribner's to complain and sometimes to cancel their subscriptions. To justify publication as catering to "popular demand" or holding "the mirror up to nature" was insufficient reason, because the vulgar mass of readers has no taste and "indecency . . . may better be unrecognized" (as one offended reader wrote).[4]

To Hemingway, this criticism was not new. Indeed, he had faced it from his own parents on the publication of his first book, *in our time,* in 1924. The copies sent them they returned with their own Victorian astonishment that their son had somehow left the pious path on which they had led him. He had defended himself in a letter to his father: "You see I'm trying in all my stories to get the feeling of the actual life across—not to just depict life—or criticize it—but to actually make it alive. . . . You can't do this without putting in the bad and the ugly as well as what is beautiful" (*Selected Letters,* 153). In a further irony, his father, seriously ill and in financial straits, had committed suicide between the time Hemingway completed *A Farewell to Arms* and Scribner published it. Hemingway's royalties from the excellent sales of the book could have assuaged his father's burdens, and he generously shared his new wealth with his widowed mother.

The best-seller status that the novel earned was encouraged by the good reviews, for the majority of the reactions were very favorable. As if in answer to Hemingway's parents' and other puritanical readers' tastes, the highly influential critic Henry Seidel Canby, writing in the very important *Saturday Review of Literature,* acknowledged that the novel was "an erotic story, shocking to the cold, disturbing to the conventional who do not like to see mere impersonal amorousness lifted into a deep, fierce love involving the best in both man and woman. . . . As for Hemingway's frankness of language, to object to it would be priggish. There is no decadence here, no overemphasis on the sexual as a philosophy" (12 October 1929). Although one might wonder what Canby meant by that last phrase, the decade of the 1920s was one of sexual liberation for some and of questioning the very nature of human sexuality to many. Freud's ideas were in the air, and if no American was as bold as he, Americans knew about the British Havelock Ellis and Marie Stopes and the Dutch Theodoor Hendrik van de Velde, whose books *The Psychology of Sex, Married Love,* and *Ideal Marriage* were frankly and practically addressing the problems of ignorance and repression.

Other influential critics, such as Malcolm Cowley and Clifton Fadiman, also wrote favorable reviews. Hemingway, after all, had just turned 30 and was still a young man. Many readers no doubt wondered if this latest book fulfilled the promise of his earlier work, which included two well-received collections of short stories and *The Sun Also Rises.* If early reviewers recognize talent and promise, later reviewers often raise their standards and demand more from a second novel than from the first. But in the cases of both Cowley and Fadiman, they felt that Hemingway had surpassed himself and written what Fadiman said was his "best book to date . . . a remarkably beautiful book . . . [and] the very apotheosis of a kind of modernism."[5]

Cowley took a different tack and saw the writing itself as "subtler and richer prose" appropriate to a changed attitude in which "emotions . . . are more colored by thought . . . [and are] more complicated" than in the earlier work.[6] Other reviewers as well often compared the new novel favorably with Hemingway's prior work, and, in view of the test of time in which, more than 60 years later, *A Farewell to Arms* continues to be so recognized, it is instructive to consider some of the details in that early critical reception.

The novel, of course, hasn't changed, except in a few editorial details, but readers' tastes and perceptions do change. What was in today is out tomorrow and vice versa, as we noted with respect to vulgate language. But other elements in the novel were early singled out for particular comment, and they continue to provide important foci for readers.

The heroine, Catherine Barkley, might be an enigma if one tried to understand her on the basis solely of criticism and not of the novel itself. Some of the early reaction to the novel found her characterization one of the best features of the work—for instance, that it "is a very fine portrayal of a woman who was not afraid."[7] But others compared her with Lady Brett Ashley, the heroine of *The Sun Also Rises*, and found her selfless devotion to and love of the hero, Frederic Henry, hard to believe. Was she not merely a man's dream-girl, little more than a farfetched, romantic pasteboard figure? The early disagreement has continued to fuel discussions, and with the rise of feminist criticism an interesting development occurred. Most of the early critics who thought many of Hemingway's women characters tended to be either male-destroying bitches or characterless dream-girls were male. Indeed, early in the new feminist movement of the 1970s Hemingway seemed to many the epitome of the macho male who regarded and depicted women as either caretakers (housekeepers, cooks, button-sewers) or sexual objects but never as thinking and feeling individuals in their own right. This feminist reaction to Hemingway was partly caused by the popular image of him, perhaps the most famous and familiar American author of all time. Photographs of him appeared on the covers and in the pages of such mass-circulation magazines as *Time* and *Life*. He was often pictured in hunting, fishing, boxing, bullfighting, or military scenes. Hollywood capitalized on and further promoted his fame as tough, hard-boiled, forcefully sexual.

Although it was certainly true that in leisure time Hemingway enjoyed many sports and as a journalist covered wars in Europe and China, he was professionally a writer, often an isolated, hardworking one. But that person, the sensitive devotee of art, was not "good press."

Stimulated by feminist criticism, notably that by Judith Fetterley in *The Resisting Reader: A Feminist Approach to American Fiction*, reexaminations of Hemingway's work took new perspectives.[8] In fact, Fetterley focused on Catherine Barkley of *A Farewell to Arms*, and in the decade since, several other books and numerous essays about Hemingway's women have been written by both men and women. Further, a posthumously published novel by Hemingway himself—*The Garden of Eden* (1986)—revealed his interest in androgyny and his ability to characterize complex male-female relations. Perhaps the only safe conclusion one can reach about Hemingway's depiction of women in general and of Catherine Barkley in particular is that it is complex, and preconceptions of Hemingway's attitudes have almost certainly impeded the careful reading and understanding of his work.

Other important questions have been raised about the novel from the very first reviews on. To what extent are the characters' feelings well depicted? Given that the novel deals with the elemental actions of war and sexuality, strong emotions are inevitable, but in art a basic principle is that the depiction of feeling should be commensurate with the source or cause of it. If such depiction is excessive or affected, we judge it to be sentimental and self-indulgent. However readers judge the balance between reason and emotion in this novel, clearly Hemingway did not shirk the risks of his subject.

Another debate opened by early reactions to *A Farewell to Arms* concerned the degree of success to which Hemingway blended the twin topics of love and war. Was this a war novel with a "romantic interest" or a love story set in wartime? If the former, some critics thought the virtual disappearance of the war from the novel's last section was a flaw. If the latter, were not the emphasis on the male's experiences for long stretches and his first-person point of view a problem?

Hemingway's friend and fellow novelist John Dos Passos would expectedly stress the craft of the novel, which he praised, but also predictably, given that his review was written for the socialist journal *New Masses,* he emphasized the political context of the novel (1 December 1929). Clearly another important and growing awareness of the protagonist, Frederic Henry, is of how the war is a class struggle, not of the Germans and Austrians versus the Italians and their allies but of the *haves* versus the *have-nots* in terms of power, money, distinction, and rank. Looked at in this way, the novel takes on yet another dimension.

One critic—who later admitted that his negative review used the novel as a whipping boy—read the book as an illustration of the psychology of behaviorism, wherein the characters, like laboratory animals, merely respond to external stimuli. They are "colorless" and "without souls," he said, and argued that although Hemingway's philosophy may echo science, it is a cruel guide to life.[9] On the other hand, charges of anti-intellectualism were raised against Hemingway. Although his characters seemed intelligent, they also seemed reluctant to think, and they evinced little culture. Wyndham Lewis's influential "The Dumb Ox: A Study of Ernest Hemingway" praised his style but criticized his primitivism, his almost-total rejection of the life of the mind.[10]

Obviously, different readers approach works of literature with different tastes, different experiences, different hopes and expectations. The richly varied responses to Hemingway's work suggest the breadth and power of the novel itself. It is not reducible to easy understanding from only one or two perspectives. Looked at from feminist, Marxist, psychological, and historical vantage points, the novel grows in our consciousness. Looked at from a narrow perspective, as it sometimes has been, the novel too narrows.

The readings of *A Farewell to Arms* that have been generous in range and that see it centrally as a work of art (and not as a polemic for or against some idea) have established it as a work of consummate writing craft, perhaps more profoundly *about* language and style themselves than about war or love. Language and its formed style are the materials with which Hemingway so carefully worked. That is not to say that this or any other novel lacks a subject and ideas; indeed, the greatness of *A Farewell to Arms* resides in part in the high seriousness of its subject of how one is to live well in a world of misrule and unreason. The vast majority of its readers have found some degree of understanding of life's dilemmas and tragedies in the well-wrought pages of this, one of the finest of modern novels.

A READING

4.

Characters

Identity

One good way of beginning to study a novel is through a consideration of its characters, for our response to the novel, our entry into it, is largely through our understanding of and degree of identification with its characters. They must interest us in fundamental ways, and we must be able to see them as somehow relevant to our own lives. In *A Farewell to Arms*, as in most novels, this relevance is indirect. We cannot, even if we wanted to, be a World War I ambulance officer or nurse's aide, but when we generalize about the kinds of characters Frederic Henry and Catherine Barkley are, we can readily identify with them and become enthralled by their story.

Noting the way in which the protagonist and narrator is *named* is in itself revealing. In chapter 1, from the very first sentence we know the story is to be told from a first-person point of view, but it is plural, not the usual singular: "*We* lived in a house" (my emphasis). Throughout that key chapter and again at the beginning of chapter 2 the narrator retains the plural *we* and *us* until, in the fifth sentence, he shifts to the singular "I," and in the mess-hall scene he engages in the conversation in "*our* mess," apparently as another officer but as one somewhat different, at least to the extent that he is neither fluent in Italian nor familiar with the places in Italy his fellow officers urge him to visit on his upcoming leave.

When the narrator returns from his leave in chapter 3, we still don't know his name, and only by chapter 4 do we learn his job in the Italian army and his rank (when one of his mechanics addresses him as "Signor Tenente"—Mr. Lieutenant). When he first meets Catherine Barkley, also in chapter 4, this curious anonymity of the narrator continues until chapter 5, when finally he is named as "Mr. Henry." His roommate, Lt. Rinaldo Rinaldi, habitually calls the narrator by a teasing or affectionate name, such as "little puppy" or "baby," and when Catherine becomes enamored of him, she regularly refers to him with such names as "darling" and "sweet." It isn't until chapter 13 that we learn his full name, Frederic Henry, and even though the novel is full of dialogue, his name is seldom mentioned.

The pattern is suggestive of an important theme in the novel, that of identity. As Frederic Henry tells us his story, he also reveals his very self, and he is an interestingly complex person, someone with whom we can readily identify. That is, he is a credible character in his own right, but he also has universal characteristics. We are drawn into his-story, but it is part of human history too.

At the beginning of the novel he is a faceless, nameless narrator, one of a group of officers and soldiers. As the plot unfolds, as he encounters other characters and develops his relationships with them (and notably with Catherine), as he acts in and reacts to various developments, he begins to change and grow. First, then, he is part of a group; then he more and more drifts away from the rest of the group as he grows in his relationship with one of the group, Catherine. Then he is almost certainly to be shot as he expects to be *mis*identified as being a member of not the group but one of the enemy. At this turning point, he breaks away and makes his famous "separate peace." He has left the *we* orientation entirely and is now free to commit himself totally to Catherine, the new "we" of only the two of them, who must then literally escape the representatives of the first "we"—the Italians and their allies—to a solitary freedom in the haven of neutral Switzerland.

Characters

A complication to their future is in the enlargement of the isolated pair through Catherine's pregnancy. The unborn baby is the new "other" that complicates their life in a different way. Now the threat to their happiness is the other person, who is ironically not an outsider but literally an insider they themselves have created through their love for each other. It will not be the bleak weather, the flooded river into which Frederic dives to escape, or any similar natural force that will end their life together; nor will it be the shells of the enemy or the bullets of the battle police. They alone, on the verge of a happy, normal life, are together brought to death by their own biology, which has led first to love and then to the stillborn baby who causes Catherine's death. Frederic, the narrator, shifts his telling of the story once more, and at the end, tragically, the varied *we*'s of the novel are now simply and solely the *I* of Frederic alone. His orientations to other people change radically, and in the process his character matures.

Clearly, his actions at the beginning of the story are those of a self-centered young man. But if we note that he himself narrates the story from a point in time *after* all the events have transpired (not day by day, as in writing a diary), we see that what he chooses to tell us about himself is selected so as to present a unified, coherent account of events and people significant to him, including, very importantly, his own self-portrait. This choice of point of view may seem "natural"—well suited to the story—but it is technically of the greatest importance. Obviously, other first-person narrators could tell of the events. Yet Catherine's experiences are different from Frederic's and are more about the nursing and behind-the-lines war. A minor character like Rinaldi could tell their story, but to contemplate such narration invites totally different novels, as does a third-person point of view in which the tale is told by a bodiless voice: "When Frederic Henry came back to the front, the officers and troops in the hospital and ambulance units still lived in Gorizia"—as a likely conversion of the beginning of chapter 3 would put it.

The novel is Frederic Henry's story, and he is writing about himself, certainly not in an egotistic but rather in a confessional way. Indeed, his story falls into a common classification of novels, the bildungsroman (literally, "education novel," or the story of one's growth or maturation). Mark Twain's *Adventures of Huckleberry Finn,* Kate Chopin's *The Awakening,* J. D. Salinger's *The Catcher in the Rye,* and Rita Mae Brown's *Rubyfruit Jungle* are other American examples of the genre. Customarily, as these other novels suggest, the protagonists are young persons, moving through adolescence to maturity or its brink. In the case of Frederic Henry, he is already in his twenties, it would seem, old enough to be on his own studying architecture in a foreign country and possessing considerable experience and wordly wisdom. He is not an innocent like Huck Finn.

Nonetheless, *A Farewell to Arms* is fundamentally a story of his education. The very title suggests his transition from one state to another, and consideration of some of the other titles Hemingway had listed confirms his awareness of this central theme in Frederic's story. Among the 30 other titles on his working list, many focused on the concept of transition in time, as *Farewell* does—for example, "Patriot's Progress," "The Time Exchanged," "Late Wisdom," and "World Enough and Time." Another group of possible titles focused more directly on the idea of education: "The Grand Tour" (referring to an extended tour of continental Europe as a climax to the education of upper-class young Englishmen), "Education of the Flesh," "The Carnal Education," and "The Sentimental Education."[11]

In one sense, in every novel there is a movement from relative ignorance to relative knowledge. Every story concludes with us readers understanding more than we did when we began the tale, and the way in which we usually define the protagonist, or chief character, is also by seeing who it is that learns. Although *A Farewell to Arms* ends bleakly, we are nonetheless left with the awareness shared with Frederic that he has grown, matured, learned. His education has been bought at a great price, but then we may value it highly because of that price.

Looking at certain stages in his education may further reveal Frederic's character. In chapter 1, notable for its description and foreshadowing, we first hear his "voice," that quality of a narrative which expresses the identity of the "speaking" character. Perhaps the concept is analogous to the scientific belief that, like our fingerprints, our voices are unique. Indeed, in chapter 1 we learn nothing about the narrator except through his voice, and at this point even to identify the voice as male is an assumption, although perhaps intuited by the sensitive reader.

What is it that we know (or think we know) about the narrator? He identifies himself with an unidentified group—"we." He is a sharp observer of human and nonhuman life and nature. He is knowledgeable about the geography and current events of his place. In the long third paragraph, he pays particular attention to the ironic juxtaposition of growth and destruction in the description of the "big guns" being camouflaged "with green branches and green leafy branches and vines" that shortly give way to the bare trees and vines of autumn, "wet and brown and dead" (4). His subtle consciousness makes another connection between the imagery of life and death (or death in the midst of life) as he describes marching soldiers with their cartridge cases of death-dealing bullets under their capes. To him they appear like pregnant women, but he chooses not to think (to write and "say") the word *pregnant* but to use the idiom "six months *gone* with child" (4; my emphasis).

Gone may also be used to mean *ruined* or *lost,* and the last two paragraphs of the chapter echo this meaning as we hear the sardonic voice of the narrator observing and commenting on first the king and the generals who lead the Italians and then the cholera epidemic. The brief chapter of only five paragraphs is remarkable in many ways, not the least of which is how it moves from the elegiac tone of the first two paragraphs, with their careful attention to detail, through the long and pivotal third paragraph, which is full of foreboding, foreshadowing imagery, with words like "dark," "guns," "night," "gray," "not successful," "fall," "fell," "bare," "black," "thin," "bare-branched," "wet and brown and dead," "muddy and wet," "heavy," "bulged," and finally "gone." The pargraph is pregnant, too, and leads to the more pronounced pessimism of the last two paragraphs.

In a carefully modulated way, the narrator moves from the expectant, elegiac notes of the first two paragraphs to heightened tension relieved by the sardonic voice he assumes at the end of the chapter. To Frederic (although he is as-yet nameless), the king is small and ineffectual, and the bountiful nature and the lovingly described river of paragraphs 1 and 2 have given way to "winter . . . the permanent rain and . . . the cholera. But it was checked and in the end only seven thousand died of it in the army" (4). The "only" is telling, for in this context it explodes to reveal, through his "voice," the dreadfully pessimistic narrator whom we sense through his foreshadowing of calamity, disclosing himself to us not, of course, with his name and rank but in the most profound and subtle way possible, taking us into his head, letting us see with his eyes, letting us hear his voice. It is a remarkable introduction to his character.

Gradually, then, we learn more about him, but always *through* him. No omniscient narrator judges or reveals him, but he does tell much about himself indirectly by his actions and by other characters' observations about him. In chapter 2 we continue to hear his sardonic voice describing the war. This chapter also encapsulates a year of the war, 1916 (as chapter 1 had summarized 1915), but the scene ending the year and the chapter is drawn out and begins to enlarge our understanding of exactly who is behind the "I" and "we." The narrator is in the officers' "bawdy house," drinking wine with another officer and watching the first snowfall of winter. His friend sees the priest-chaplain passing by and "motioned for him to come in," but understandably the priest "went on" (6). Presumably Frederic's friend's gesture was in the same spirit of the baiting of the young priest that amuses all the officers of the mess that night as they dine. In both scenes, Frederic looks on and is passive. His only judgments are of the dinner: all the officers eat the spaghetti "very quickly and seriously," and Frederic describes the wine as "clear red, tannic and lovely" (7). The sentence is remarkable stylistically and psychologically. It begins by relegating the spaghetti course at dinner to an adverbial modifier, but the spaghetti and the wine take over the long and strangely structured sentence until, almost as an afterthought, Frederic concludes the sentence with the main clause: "the captain commenced picking on the priest" (7). That is, although he wants to go on telling us about the baiting, he does that neutrally. The food and wine are sensuously described, however, and we see Frederic as a creature of appetite, an appetite that includes the one satisfied in the whorehouse, to which presumably he goes at the end of the chapter on the invitation of the coarse captain.

At the beginning of chapter 2, Frederic's voice is sardonic when he describes the town Gorizia as having been "captured very handsomely" and the war being fought as a game when he notes "the Austrians seemed to want to come back to the town some time, if the war should end, because they did not bombard it to destroy it but only a little in a military way" (5). And again, "the whole thing"—almost cruelly meaning the fighting—"going well" reveals his own self-contempt, as well as his perception of the mindless, inhuman way he and presumably many others had come to think of the war (6).

But at the end of the chapter, in the dining scene, we perceive more of his character from what he does and doesn't do. Mainly, he passively listens as the other officers tell crude jokes about the priest and his religion. The priest emerges as a modest, tolerant, sensitive, kind man who gracefully endures the baiting and offers Frederic both an invitation to visit his family when he goes on leave and, through his behavior, an alternative model of response to one's situation in life: on the one hand, the officers; on the other, the priest. At this point we don't know precisely what values each represents, but the conversation here makes the difference of choice very clear. The officers urge Frederic to spend his leave pursuing culture, civilization, and sex. In an ironic argument over the bellowing or singing of Caruso, the officers themselves are shouting, while beneath the din the priest describes his homeland, where Frederic could pursue game and not women and where he could stay with the priest's family. Frederic's choice is foreshadowed by his saying goodnight to the priest and going with the captain to the whorehouse.

That is, although he perceives another way of living, another way of responding to the war and his small role in it, Frederic chooses the path of immediate sensual pleasure. He and the priest smile knowingly at each other; perhaps the priest has sensed in Frederic values that make him worth trying to reach, to offer an alternative to the way of the flesh. But although Frederic is attracted to the priest, when he returns from his leave (chapter 3) he reticently but without remorse tells his friend and roommate, Lt. Rinaldi, of his "magnificent" leave: "I went everywhere" (11). But in the next scene, when he tells the priest about his leave, he does so in a totally different spirit. Indeed, he did not go "everywhere," for he had not gone to the remote mountain region of the Abruzzi to stay with the priest's family, "where it was clear cold and dry and the snow was dry and powdery and hare-tracks in the snow and the peasants took off their hats and called you Lord and there was good hunting" (13).

For an intelligent, articulate narrator capable of vivid and moving descriptions, even imagined ones like this sentence about the unseen Abruzzi, Frederic seldom reveals his innermost self. Thus here at the end of chapter 3 his revelation is important even though ambiguous and merely foreshadowing a more complete revelation later on. For one thing, his apology to the hurt priest who had invited him to his home is given "winefully" after "much wine" and an after-dinner drink of Strega. Surely he is mocking his own behavior when he defensively and in a maudlin tone "explained" that "[we never did] the things we wanted to do" (13). Then in the next paragraph, beginning with his attractive evocation of the Abruzzi, he goes on in even greater detail, recollecting what it was he *had* done on his leave, indulging his appetite for drink and women night after night. In short, he is like many human beings, recognizing two ways of behavior, morally desiring the better one, but often yielding to that "strange excitement" of the flesh. Like faith, this excitement too has an element of mystery, and Frederic concedes that he "tried to tell [the priest] about the night . . . and I could not tell it; as I cannot tell it now. But if you have had it you know. He had not had it" (13).

This passage, with its striking use of the repeated and somewhat-ambiguous pronoun *it*—presumably referring in a general way to the "strange excitement" of his indulgent life—contrasts with an even more ambiguous use of *it* that immediately follows. If the priest did not know the "strange excitement," he does know something that

Frederic is yet to learn: "He had always *known* what I did *not know* and what, when I *learned it,* I was always able to forget. But I did *not know* that then, although I *learned it* later" (14; my emphasis). Coming early in the novel after the setting of the stage of the unfolding drama, this key passage directly tells us that the story will be about some kind of education of the narrator and protagonist, Frederic Henry, and that it is likely to be about the difference between the way of life represented by the cynical, faithless officers and the ideals represented by the priest. At this point in the story we can only infer those ideals from the priest's manners in contrast to the behavior of the officers, but his ideals will gradually emerge during the course of Frederic's narration of his own "education."

By the end of the novel, Frederic has changed greatly and in many ways. He changes from an architecture student who has without much thought joined the Italian army; he deserts the army after some thought and deadly provocation and escapes to neutral Switzerland. He changes from a self-indulgent, unattached young man to someone who accepts the love of Catherine Barkley and assumes responsibility for their shared life together, including the impending birth of their child. From being carefree and manipulative of a vulnerable, attractive woman (in short, in being despicable and irresponsible), he becomes loving and caring, sensitive to Catherine's feelings and needs. He also comes to view the war and the people in it in very different ways. To him the war is no longer like a game between two sides—as in sports, striving for victories and suffering from losses. He himself was severely wounded, he witnessed the deaths of some of his own men whom he liked, he shot a sergeant for disobeying his order, he himself was nearly executed, and he deserted and made his "separate peace." Both his personal and his public lives have been greatly changed, and at the end of the novel he is left with nothing, as the private life with Catherine that had grown and replaced the public life of the soldier is taken away from him: first farewell to the arms of war; then farewell to the arms of Catherine. First, love and responsibility for Catherine; then, if not love and responsibility for others, at least the dawning of a new understanding of how he must live in a world that is in many ways mad with unreason and cruelty, lacking the comforting design of neither man nor god. It is a bleak ending, but it leaves us nevertheless with something like the cathartic feelings of tragedy. The great have been brought low, but in their fall from pride and strength we yet feel the potential nobility of human beings who face adversity with courage and grace.

Vital Statistics

If asked to characterize ourselves, many of us might begin with the sort of information typically found on an application form, and thinking about Frederic Henry and Catherine Barkley in this way might at first be enlightening. Name, sex, age, address? Marital status, occupation, religion, nationality, citizenship status, race? Memberships or interests in social, political, educational, religious, athletic organizations? What of one's family—parents, siblings? Their occupations and where-abouts? Even by the end of *A Farewell to Arms,* however, we know remarkably little about the two chief characters in these common regards.

Hemingway on occasion described an aesthetic principle of his as analogous to an iceberg, seven-eighths of which is concealed beneath the surface of the water in which it floats. A good writer does not need to reveal every detail of a character or action; the one-eighth that is presented will suggest all other meaningful dimensions of the story.

Thus, Hemingway may not introduce information that can be easily inferred from details that are given. For example, because Frederic Henry, the narrator, is a careful observer of *some* details, we infer that he is a careful observer; however, if we have some degree of healthy skepticism we do not infer that he is a careful observer of *all* details. In chapter 1, that key point of departure, we first meet (or "hear" the voice of) the narrator. Can one recall one's thoughts and feelings on first reading that chapter? Once having read the novel, we cannot innocently return to it, because the matter of the subsequent chapters (remembered imperfectly, no doubt) will color our rereading. Still, it would be an interesting and perhaps a revealing experiment to test the impact and judge the significance of that first chapter alone before readers went on to the rest of the novel.

In terms of basic questions—the "vital statistics" of the characters—we discover that chapter 1 tells us nothing about anyone in particular. We hear a virtually disembodied voice who speaks for a plural "we" who "lived in a house" in an unnamed "village" in an unidentified "year" on an unidentified "river" that is then carefully described. We infer that the narrator, who also carefully describes marching soldiers, is in close contact with the people and events of war, but we can have only a general idea that it is a modern war (because of the motor transport referred to) and that it is probably European because of the detailed description of the vegetation and the terrain and the fact that the ruler is a king. If our geographic knowledge is acute or if we have an atlas at hand, we can confirm some of our inferences from the sole specific reference to the city of Udine, in northeast Italy.

This reticence about vital statistics runs throughout the novel and continues to suggest the relevance of Hemingway's iceberg theory. But it also, and perhaps more significantly, draws our attention to the way in which the story is told. That is, Frederic Henry is the main character; he is also the all-important narrator, the filter through which comes everything the reader knows. That filter, as the image suggests, *takes out* (leaves concealed, like the iceberg) just as surely as it articulates or gives us information. And we will read well to the degree that we are alert to *how* the story is being told.

We are well into the novel before we learn a name for the narrator—"Mr. Henry" (25)—and readers not knowing that *tenente* is Italian for "lieutenant" are understandably led to think that the narrator's name may be Henry Tenente. The badinage about his name in Italian at the officers' mess furthers the intended or functional confusion; it is a meaningful ambiguity about the narrator's very identity that becomes central to his story. Was his name "Frederico Enrico or Enrico Federico?" (40). This is the first clue we have to his given name, and in one other bibulous exchange, an officer calls him Federico (76–77). But not until the beginning of book 2 of the novel do we learn it by his response to the nurse's direct question:

> "What's your name?"
> "Henry. Frederic Henry." (84)

Indeed, afterward occurs no other reference to his full name and only several to his last name. He himself at one point introduces himself with an Italianate form of his last name, "Tenente Enry" (97). Remarkably, the people who are fond of him and regularly talk with him (Catherine, Rinaldo, the priest, his soldiers) never use his first name but refer to him by his rank (the soldiers) or by affectionate general names like "baby" (Rinaldo) and "darling" (Catherine).

Other vital statistics are equally obscure or minimally noted. At several places in the novel, Frederic Henry discusses religion with the priest (also nameless) and Count Greffi (chapter 35), to whom he confesses that he "might become very devout" and that he will pray for the Count (263). At the end of the novel, when Catherine is dying, he recalls a camping incident in which he had "a splendid chance to be a messiah" and save some ants from being burned, but he did not. Now, as his beloved desperately needs saving, his fervent prayers for her are futile: "Dear God, don't let her die" (330). Indeed, religion is significant throughout the novel, whether in the character of the priest or in the absence of religion in the lives of most of the other characters. Catherine gives Frederic a Saint Anthony's medal meant to protect him, but he is severely wounded anyhow and later discovers the medal was stolen (43–44). Before Passini, one of his ambulance drivers, dies from the same mortar round that wounds him, Passini repeatedly and futilely prays to Jesus and Mary in a foreshadowing of Frederic's equally futile prayers for Catherine (55). We do know that she is "not a Catholic," but she nonetheless thinks the Saint Anthony's medal will protect Frederic (43). And we never learn what her or Frederic's religion is, that is, the sort of identification one gives in filling out forms. Indeed, although one might infer that the nominal faith of the characters in predominantly Catholic Italy would be Catholic, the two chief characters are foreigners, and the only character almost certainly Catholic is the priest. And "almost certainly" is not an entirely exaggerated caution in regard to a novel in which the uncertainty and insecurity of life are omnipresent. The central theme is thus promoted by the lack of clear-cut identifications of the characters' vital statistics.

We know that Catherine's nationality is Scottish, not English, but to the Italians, the distinction is remote and unclear. What are Frederic's profession and reason for serving in the Italian army? So frequently we categorize and even stereotype persons by their occupation: What do you *do*? Early on we learn that Frederic is in the Italian army because at the outbreak of the war he was in Italy and he spoke Italian (22). The cause-effect relationship is comic, absurd, but no more so than the illogic of many other decisions in the novel. There is no awareness or consciousness of significant moral, social, or political reasons for his decisions and actions that eventually become life-threatening. Frederic chooses as casually as one might choose what to order from a menu. But what does he *do*? Not until late in the novel do we learn that Frederic "wanted to be an architect" (242). He repeats the claim when he and Catherine are entering Switzerland—"I have been studying architecture" (280)—but apart from his assertion he says and does nothing in particular to support it. In short, it seems to be of little significance to him.

Yet one other common source of identity, in and through one's family, is notably absent from the novel. Is it likely that one could write an entire book about several important years in one's lifetime, including an intense love affair with another person, and yet write nothing about one's immediate family or the family of one's beloved? Frederic Henry virtually succeeds, for we have to read carefully to discover the few details linking either him or Catherine to their families. They are totally deracinated, seldom communicating with or even thinking of parents, siblings, or homes, at least as far as Frederic's narrative is concerned. In lieu of real homes, Catherine and Frederic make "homes" of his room in the hospital (153) and in three hotels, one in Milan before he returns to the battlefront, one in Stresa after he has deserted the army and rejoined Catherine, and the last in Lausanne, where they go to await the birth of their baby (155, 249, 309).

The first hotel, near the railroad station, caters to illicit lovers and casual sexual encounters. The behavior of Frederic in picking that particular hotel and its description tell us as much. He and Catherine are unmarried and without luggage; they would not be welcome in a respectable hotel like the Cavour. "They wouldn't have taken us in there," Frederic tells Catherine, who had at first been offended by the obsequious behavior of the hotel manager and by the whorehouse decor. But after they dine and presumably make love, her unhappiness fades and Frederic asserts, "[W]e felt very happy and in a little time the room felt like our own home," as had his hospital room earlier. Even Catherine settles in and somewhat humorously accepts the decor—"But it's really a splendid room"—and she too refers to it as "our home" (152–55).

Within this passage another exchange between them focuses on their families, "back home," and it is the only time in the novel in which Catherine specifically mentions her own family. (Earlier we learn that her home is in Scotland and that her supervising nurse, Miss Van Campen, thinks "Catherine came from very good people"; 115, 118.) In response to Frederic's observation on the goodness of wine, Catherine agrees and then adds, "But it's given my father gout very badly." Frederic's responding question, "Have you a father?" is at once absurd and revelatory, as is Catherine's affirmative response, followed by "You won't ever have to meet him. Haven't you a father?"

In a literal sense, Frederic's answer is as absurd as his and Catherine's questions: no, he doesn't have a father; he has a stepfather. And he repeats almost exactly Catherine's words: "You won't have to meet him" (154).

What this exchange dramatically reveals is the depth of their isolation even before they become further alienated from society when Frederic deserts the army and they flee to Switzerland and live in isolation there. Of course, both of them assume that the other has a family, at least a biological one. But here, halfway through the narrative, they discuss for the first time the existence of their families, and instead of recognizing their future life together as involving mutual family interaction, they both unrealistically pledge that the other will not even have to meet the father and stepfather, let alone others in their families, and share the usual social activities with them.

When Frederic then returns to the army, to his duty, to his social responsibility, "It did not feel like a homecoming" (163), for now he, like Catherine, has made his "home" with the other. Thus, when he deserts the army and rejoins her in Stresa, he takes another hotel room; Catherine ditches her friend Helen Ferguson (the representative of a broader, more usual social life); and the lovers for the second time feel "we had come home" in the utterly new environment of a hotel room (249).

Similarly, three weeks before Catherine dies, when they move into the last room they will share, she declines Frederic's telling her to come to bed with him by saying she must first make their room look "like our home" (309). At work perhaps is her maternal nesting instinct, for Frederic does not similarly report his feelings for the room; nor does he help her settle in. (He doesn't even help her unpack.) They had gone to Montreux, where they knew no one and where the only person they had come to know was Catherine's hair-dresser (292). Then they move to Lausanne, where they "can be . . . alone" in their final days together, in their last "home" (307). Inasmuch as Frederic is the narrator and main character, it is unsurprising that we learn somewhat more about his family than we do about Catherine's (in her case, we learn only that her home is in Scotland and her father has gout). But we learn precious little nonetheless, and again Frederic's deracination is emphasized. We have already noted that he has a stepfather but no acknowledged father. Throughout the novel Frederic calls the important minor character, the priest, "father," although he is young and inexperienced. As the narrator, Frederic records another instance that makes light of his paternity: when he is wounded, an English ambulance driver assists in Frederic's care by telling the field-hospital attendants first that "He is the legitimate son of President Wilson" and then that he is "The only son of the American Ambassador" (58–59).

Occasional passing references to his family stress his alienation from it. When Frederic is about to go to the battlefront he recalls that for "a long time" he hasn't "written to the States" (he doesn't even say to "my family" or "my mother," and indeed the novel contains not a single reference to his mother). In lieu of writing, he sends a couple of postcards with preprinted messages, selecting from them one saying, "I am well" (36). Later we learn that he seems to have a closer relationship with a grandfather than with anyone else in his family, for in a drunken conversation he reveals that he can cash drafts of money from his grandfather's account (76), and the only letter he acknowledges receiving from his family is from the grandfather, "containing family news, patriotic encouragement, a draft for two hundred dollars, and a few clippings" (135). Notable here is the sardonic edge of "patriotic encouragement" and the very large amount of money (by 1917 standards). There are casual references to a grandmother (258) and to "my relatives" who used to send him tobacco (244). Catherine, it seems, thinks family ties are more important than Frederic does. When he is to be operated on and she is afraid that under anesthesia he might babble of their intimacy, she advises him to "think about your people" (103). More significant is the exchange between them in Switzerland after so much drama has transpired and she learns that he hasn't written his family but has only drawn money on them:

> "Thank God I'm not your family [she tells him with some irony]. Don't you care anything about them?"
> "I did, but we quarrelled so much it wore itself out." (304)

With no factual basis for the remark, Catherine says she thinks she would like his family "very much." This belief must stem from an extrapolation of her knowledge of Frederic, a kind of enthymeme in which she reasons that since Frederic is so lovable his family must be too. Here then Frederic reveals a chink in his apparent indifference to his family: "Let's not talk about them or I'll start to worry about them" (304). The exchange is in a way astonishing, but on reflection it reveals something basic to his nature; we'll return to it as a theme that runs throughout the novel of a fear of thinking about difficult matters. In another passage the venerable Count Greffi states a feeling that Frederic remembered in his retelling of this momentous year in his life: "one misses one's countrymen and especially one's countrywomen" (260). This remark, though not Frederic's, is adumbrated in some moments of reflection during his retreat when, for the single instance in the novel, Frederic reveals a specific event in his past life. Because it is so unusual it must have unusual meaning to him (and to us readers).

One of his drivers has just been killed, and he is in the midst of the chaos of a disorganized army's retreat before an advancing, menacing enemy. Shortly he himself will face death and make a momentous decision to desert the army. He is lying in sweet-smelling hay on a barn floor, waiting for his other drivers, who are foraging for food and waiting for darkness to cover their retreat: "The hay smelled good and lying in a barn in the hay took away all the years in between. We had lain in hay and talked and shot sparrows with an air rifle when they perched in the triangle cut high up in the wall of the barn. The barn was gone now and one year they had cut the hemlock woods and there were only stumps, dried tree-tops, branches and fireweed where the woods had been. You could not go back" (216). There his reverie ends, and he returns to thoughts of his present predicament. This solitary reminiscence of the past, triggered by his presence in a similar setting, suggests deeply ingrained feelings. The ambiguous *we* and *they* of the passage ("*we* had lain," "*they* had cut"), never explained, are like the *we* and *they* of the current action or the world simplistically divided into good guys and bad guys. Throughout the novel Frederic has described the vegetation (especially trees) of the landscape. It is significant to him not merely because of any practical value but also because, as revealed here, of its psychological association with his past, presumably (since "we" had an air rifle) his youth. To what could he not go back? Presumably his youth and the comfort of home. Literally, of course, one cannot go back in time, but Frederic's reflections here reveal an elegiac attitude toward life that is also fatalistic. Once upon a time, life was better, but the literal and figurative trees are inevitably cut down by *them*. While one may elegiacally remember the past, the figurative "home," one can never return to it. As Thomas Wolfe, Hemingway's contemporary, later put it in the title of one of his novels, *You Can't Go Home Again* (1940).

The critic Harold Bloom has suggested that the elegiac mood or attitude toward life is dominant in American literature, and not just in obvious elegies, such as Walt Whitman's "When Lilacs Last in the Dooryard Bloom'd," in which Whitman laments the death of Abraham Lincoln.[12] Ingrained in the American character, as in Frederic Henry, is a longing for something irrevocably lost, and the natural landscape is often a physical image of what is lost spiritually or psychologically. In war, the cannons have blasted the trees: "The forest of oak trees . . . was gone. The forest had been green . . . but now there were the stumps and the broken trunks and the ground torn up" (6). *They* will cut you down, one way or another. "Stay around and they would kill you" (327)—the theme is held together from the beginning of the novel to the end by the quietly persistent presence of the imagery of growth and destruction in the landscape. Yes, the world has "many thick shady trees in a walled garden and a wistaria vine purple on the side of the house" (5), and Hemingway's writing here and elsewhere is full of such description that measures his joy in the physical world. But *they*, and we Americans especially, are careless of that natural world in its beauty, of our once "home," and in one breath we both praise it and lament its loss. (See, for instance, the opening of Hemingway's short story "Big Two-Hearted River" and the last chapter of *Green Hills of Africa*, in which he contrasts the relatively unblighted Africa of 50 years ago with blighted America.) Right after this exceptional reverie in the barn, Frederic and his driver are marching in the column of retreating soldiers, many of whom hope that the war is over, and if Frederic cannot go home to that "lost America of love" (in Allen Ginsberg's words), the soldiers repeatedly shout, "We're going home. . . . *Andiamo a casa*!"[13] Frederic's driver picks up on the idea: " 'It would be fine if we all went home,' Piani said. 'Wouldn't you like to go home?' "

Frederic answers, simply, "Yes" (219).

Characters

Frederic Henry

In a later chapter on themes, we will look closely at the several passages in the novel wherein characters (notably Frederic) think or express thoughts that reveal their knowledge and beliefs. *Character*, after all, means one's moral or ethical identity as well as being a neutral, nonjudgmental term for a person in a play or story. As shown in the preceding section, we must infer much of Frederic's moral and ethical nature, for he rarely tells us directly what that is. In any case, in most good literature as in life, the adage "Action speaks louder than words" is a good one to bear in mind. Hearing the pledge of a Faust who sells his soul to the Devil in exchange for worldly pleasure and power is not in itself sufficient basis (extreme though it is) for a judgment on Faust's character. What does he then *do* with his life? Neither is hearing the pledge of an elected official to uphold the Constitution and the law enough to make a character judgment *or a story*. For that we need action, deeds.

In the case of our main character, his deeds *characterize* him as a protagonist rather than a hero. Indeed, one central feature (or *characteristic*) of modern life and literature is the dearth of traditional heroes and heroines, persons of unusual courage and strength who act boldly in behalf of their friends and allies. In classical literature they were often the children of one mortal and one divine parent, and thus their deeds were often favored by the gods. In more recent literature, as in the novels of Walter Scott, Jane Austen, Emily Brontë, and Nathaniel Hawthorne, a hero or heroine was still bold, noble, and courageous and often one who sacrificed one's power or even life for others.

Thinking of Frederic Henry in these terms seems inappropriate. Even though he has some characteristics of the traditional hero, several of his most important actions (or inactions) lead us to conclude that he might better be designated as an antihero, a protagonist who significantly lacks key heroic qualities. This is not to say that to most readers he is unsympathetic. Indeed, we can perhaps more readily identify with him and understand his feelings, thoughts, and actions because he is not heroic, is not remote, as is an Achilles, a Hercules, or even a George Washington, whose character continues to fascinate and elude biographers. But some readers of the novel have reached conclusions very unsympathetic to Frederic, and these analyses too should be heeded.

Considering his character in outline, one might conclude that Frederic has heroic qualities. His strength is evidenced in several key episodes. The first is his survival of the artillery bombardment that kills one of his men in the same dugout. Though hit badly, he generously offers to let others be treated before him. Then he fully recovers from his wounds, and in a few months he even more dramatically illustrates his strength by running from his captors, diving fully clothed into a flooded river, and perilously swimming to safety. A third demonstration of his prowess occurs at yet another turning point, when, briefly spelled by Catherine, he rows a boat all night long for more than 20 miles in their escape to Switzerland.

His courage is likewise demonstrated in this episode, as it is earlier in the stress of the hazardous retreat. He is fully aware of the dangers from both the enemy and the Italians, who mistake him and his drivers for Germans, kill one of them, and then threaten to summarily try and execute Frederic. His escape is an act of derring-do worthy of a true hero, and it comes as no surprise. We are quite ready to accept the episode as in keeping with his character. At the same time, we realize that his options are limited. He faces possible death of the sort he has just witnessed with the little lieutenant colonel, who behaves with dignity, displaying religious faith and moral if not physical courage. Frederic also witnesses the trial of the next officer, who, unlike the first one, breaks down. Frederic thus has seen two alternatives for himself in the face of what he figures is certain death. He could confront the sanctimonious battle police, argue his case, present his identification papers, suggest that the death of an American volunteer would get them in trouble and perhaps ruin their careers; he could suggest that they detain him until his story could be verified. But such behavior would not be *in character;* it would instead, I believe, surprise us, had Hemingway so chosen to rewrite the novel. This critical episode has been foreshadowed by other ones of less drama but still of tension between Frederic and others, and in them he typically conceals his real thoughts or says nothing at all. Suddenly to become an articulate and persuasive defender of his life and views at this point would be out of character. Right before this episode with the battle police, when his last driver, Piani, tells him of Bonello's desertion, Frederic twice notes, "I did not say anything" (217)—just as earlier, in a crucial scene with his assistant, Gino, whose patriotic talk is embarrassing to Frederic, he states, "I did not say anything" (184). Even in a casual, happy talk with Catherine before his operation his reticence is illustrated; he "won't talk" under anesthesia and embarrass Catherine (104). Of course, he talks throughout the novel, but in moments of crisis he is remarkably reticent. Whether in the arms of swelling Catherine when he tells her, "Don't talk" (92) or beside the swollen Tagliamento, he will not talk but plunge in.

In terms of other characteristics of traditional heroes, we similarly find that Frederic has related but different qualities.

Hero	Frederic the Antihero
Courage (moral and physical)	Physical courage
Strength	Strength
Boldness	Boldness
Favored by gods	Ultimately crushed by gods (fate)
Nobility	Commonplaceness
Sacrificer and protector	Selfish
Craft	Crafty
Actor	Reactor

Of course, this dualism is dangerous if one pushes it to an either-or trap, and it groups Frederic with considerably lesser antiheroes, such as Theodore Dreiser's Clyde Griffith (in *An American Tragedy*) and Richard Wright's Bigger Thomas (in *Native Son*). Given different circumstances—such as a war that was not so dreadfully ambiguous as the Great War—we might well imagine Frederic as more traditionally heroic. His selfishness, for instance, is not absolute, and until he is driven to desert he is remarkably dutiful and loyal to the army. But he has neither the position of a king or general nor the heroic qualities of an otherwise-ordinary person like a Joan of Arc. If not an Everyman figure, he is still more like most of us than he is like a hero. Nor is he notably successful in his role as a protector of the wounded. True, he did volunteer for service in the Italian army ambulance corps before his own country became involved in the war, but his motivation seems to have been weak. When Catherine asks him, "Why did you join up with the Italians?" he replies, "I was in Italy, . . . and I spoke Italian" (22). This service includes relaxed, comfortable quarters; leaves that last all winter; and the congenial company of fellow officers and the inhabitants of the officers' bordello. On returning from leave in the spring of 1917, he notes that his ambulance unit is "in good condition," and he twice observes that he is irrelevant, unnecessary, hardly a sacrificer or protector: "It evidently made no difference whether I was there to look after things or not . . ." (16). "The whole thing seemed to run better while I was away" and now that he's back, he has only "a false feeling of soldiering" (17).

Given actual chances to help people, he, like a hero, tries but, unlike a hero, fails: in chapter 7, Frederic tries to help the ruptured soldier who wants out of the war, but the ruse they agree to, in which the soldier injures himself, doesn't work (33–36).

Soon thereafter, Frederic does manage to get some food for himself and his drivers. But while they are eating they are blown up by a huge trench mortar shell. Wounded himself, Frederic attempts to apply a tourniquet to the leg of the driver, Passini; however, he dies before Frederic can save him (55), just as another soldier hemorrhages to death in an ambulance and Frederic tries to but cannot aid him (61). These episodes foreshadow Frederic's ultimate failure and helplessness at the end of the novel, when Catherine also hemorrhages to death. He may give her gas to ease her pain, but even that activity, as he recognizes when he notes, "It was very good of the doctor to let me do something" (317), is minimal and for his benefit, not solely Catherine's.

Other episodes in which Frederic's desired role as protector and benefactor is frustrated occur when he gets Catherine pregnant, having often thought of his own pleasure but having never thought of the consequences for her of a pregnancy. The confrontation in the railway car when he is returning to the front is similar; he uses his rank and money to save himself a seat on the crowded train and relinquishes it to the "tall gaunt captain . . . with a red scar along his jaw" only when he faces the hostility as well as the superior virtue of the captain (158–59). Later on the retreat he fails to carry out his mission even though he strives mightily to do so. His ambulances and their loads of hospital equipment are lost, one of his drivers is killed, and one deserts. The one who remains with him changes somewhat the roles of the leader and the led: the reason Piani did not desert is that he did not want to leave Frederic alone (217); moreover, he forages food for them and takes Frederic "by the arm" and warns him of danger as they cross the bridge (219). They are more equals than not. The hitchhikers they had earlier picked up to help them too escape are indeed not helped. The two young sisters are virtually terrorized and are relieved when the ambulances (vehicles of mercy) are stuck in the mud and they are allowed to rejoin the main column of the retreat. The two sergeants they have picked up fare even less well in Frederic's role as protector. Not entirely without reason—indeed, with the very reason Frederic himself will soon invoke when he deserts, *survival*—the sergeants leave the stuck ambulances, refusing to help dislodge them, and Frederic shoots one of them. Albeit one of the sergeants' manners had been offensive to Frederic and his drivers, shooting them seems draconian justice and an ironic precursor of Frederic's desertion. The act is the nadir of his failed role as leader and protector, and he so acknowledges "It was my fault" (205) and "I had failed at that" (212).

One final episode in this vein of failed hero occurs when Catherine is in labor, and although it might seem inconsequential, Frederic apparently felt it worth citing: "A dog was nosing at one of the [refuse] cans," and Frederic, once more trying to be a benefactor (literally a *do-gooder*) fails. He finds "nothing on top but coffee-grounds, dust and some dead flowers. 'There isn't anything, dog,' " he says, in a powerful image of failure, loss, and death (315).

Another principal difference between the hero and the antihero is illustrated in the main characters of Homer's old tales *Iliad* and

Odyssey. In the former, also a tale of love and war, the hero, Achilles, is traditional in his strength and courage and the *craft* of the warrior. In *Odyssey* the protagonist is Odysseus, who has many traditional heroic qualities but whose character significantly changes craft to *crafty.* Above all else, Odysseus survives and achieves victory because of his guile, his shrewdness, his ability to emerge from danger through his quick wit. At the beginning of *A Farewell to Arms* we first see this central trait demonstrated by Frederic in his relations with his fellow officers, who range from the gentle priest to the bawdy and rude captain. In the episode in the officers' mess (chapter 2), Frederic is remarkably passive and reports only two lines of his own dialogue in the entire chapter (half of which is mainly dialogue). One line is simply " 'Good-night,' I said to the priest" (9); the other is a neutral, factual observation: " 'There will be no more offensive now that the snow has come,' I said" (8).

One can look at these lines in at least two significant ways. On the one hand, they are entirely conventional statements that enable the speaker to remain neutral in the coarse jesting and the officers' arguments (no doubt slightly fueled by the dinner wine). Frederic neither sides with the captain baiting the priest nor defends the priest. Moreover, he does not take sides in the arguments about religion and atheism, the Free Masons, and where he should go on his upcoming leave. He does once communicate silently with the priest when they exchange smiles, and thus he stays in favor with both sides, listening to and not objecting to the baiting but letting the priest know through his smile that he sympathizes with him. The priest's smile and response to Frederic, "Don't you read it" (8)—meaning the antichurch book *The Black Pig*—would seem to confirm that the priest too thinks he has found in Frederic a sympathetic friend.

On the other hand, these two lines of Frederic's dialogue bear other meaning in that the imagery of weather and particularly the contrasting associations of snow and rain form a motif running throughout the novel. The even briefer "Good-night" to the priest, in context, reveals that although Frederic may be crafty, his decision here seems to have been to "take sides," to leave the priest, who has just urged him to visit his family, and to join the captain in going to the whorehouse. This tension between Frederic's attractions to (a) the priest and his values and (b) the pleasures of the flesh is confirmed in the next chapter when he returns from leave, sits next to the priest, but reveals that rather than realizing the hopes of the priest he instead indulged his carnal appetites.

The pattern continues when Frederic meets Catherine Barkley, finds her "very beautiful" (18, 26), and sets out to seduce her. His tactics are deliberate and clever; they are not noble or heroic. He does not win over Catherine by his courage in battle or in tournament, as a traditional hero would, becoming like an Othello or Ivanhoe his lady's champion. When Catherine slaps him, *resisting* his *advances* (the language of love being remarkably parallel to the language of battle), he deceitfully *retreats* and *camouflages* his anger by acknowledging (*propagandizing?*), "You did exactly right. . . . I don't mind at all." Instead, he feels he "had a certain advantage" when she apologizes, and he sees "it all ahead like the moves in a chess game" (26). Although the "it" here has no antecedent, we clearly know to what Frederic refers, the convention of love as a kind of *game* in which the aggressor tries to subdue, seduce, or rape the other person. (The military concept of "playing war games" draws the three fields of battle—love, war, and game [or sport]—together in our vocabulary.) Frederic's bold frontal attack on Catherine having been warded off, he resorts to trickery and uses his superior knowledge of the psychology of love to *get around* Catherine.

Taken in context, his "line" is outrageous, for he is "still angry" as she consents to kiss him and finally yields to his aggressive kiss. But his combination of deceitful self-pity and flattery works perfectly. His response to her yielding is his cruel thought, "What the hell," revealing both his cynicism and his immorality (27). Three days later he goes courting again, explains why he hasn't communicated with her in the interim, and resumes his campaign to seduce her. Catherine asks,

> "And you do love me?"
> "Yes."

"You did say you loved me, didn't you?"
"Yes," I lied. "I love you." I had not said it before. (30)

The vulnerable Catherine, recovering from the death of her fiancé in the war, seeks assurance of Frederic's seriousness of purpose. He readily lies and leads her on, kissing her with his eyes open, hers closed, thinking she is "a little crazy" but also thinking a casual loveless affair with her is better than "going every evening" to the officers' whorehouse. Again he compares their romance to a game, this time not to chess but to bridge, and his next thought is of finding a comfortable place to make love. In turn, the sensitive Catherine reveals that she too perceives the sham courtship to be "a rotten game" (31) and that Frederic has been lying. Nevertheless, she values his companionship and says he is "very nice" and "a very good boy," as the priest had (31).

Something subtly important takes place. After this transition to honesty and openness, Frederic again wants to kiss her, and Catherine accedes. After they part, Frederic returns to his quarters and passes the officers' whorehouse, still in revelry, but he returns to his solitary bed. The next day, after his duty he fantasizes about an assignation with Catherine and intends to visit her that evening. But at the evening mess he drinks too much, and when he finally goes to call on Catherine she is indisposed and won't see him. The crafty seducer no more, he regrets taking Catherine lightly and feels "lonely and hollow" (41). Before he goes off the next day to his nearly fatal wounding, he briefly greets her, and she gives him a Saint Anthony's medal for protection. It is the last time they will see each other for nearly a week (covering five chapters, 9–13), and when they are reunited, as soon as he sees her, he is "in love with her. . . . God knows I had not wanted to fall in love with her. . . . But God knows I had" (91, 93).

In a crucial sense, then, Frederic's relationship with Catherine has become less immoral than it was. Although his love to a degree legitimizes his passion, he nevertheless continues to pursue the satisfaction of his lust in a crafty way, and despite his wounding they begin making love in his hospital bed. (He satisfies another taste, for alcoholic drink, in a covert way as well until the head nurse finds out about his drinking [chapter 22].) His craftiness does not extend to birth control, however, and not unsurprisingly Catherine becomes pregnant.

Catherine's innocence contrasts with Frederic's experience and shrewdness on their last night together in Milan. Although he backs down from his trick to save himself a seat on the crowded train (chapter 24), the prior episode well demonstrates his worldly wisdom and craftiness. Of course Catherine wishes to be alone with Frederic during their last hours together, but it is he who knows that the hotel near the railroad station will not stand on ceremony or inhibit the sin of fornication. But Frederic ensures them against embarrassment by preceding Catherine and discretely talking to the manager, who, with "plenty of rooms" on his hands (151) and a policy of prepayment from strangers (156), somewhat obsequiously ushers them to their overdecorated room. The hotel is not a whorehouse, but the red plush, the chandelier (glass, not crystal), the large satin-covered bed, and the "many mirrors"—as well as the manager's behavior—reveal it to Catherine as a place of illicit assignations. Thus, she is initially depressed—"I never felt like a whore before"—and Frederic is frustrated, thinking selfishly that his night of love will be spoiled. "Oh, hell, I thought, do we have to argue now?" (152). Since we know that Frederic had previously caroused in Milan and that the hotel manager "remembered [him] as a friend" (156), we can assume Frederic had brought actual whores to the hotel. No doubt Catherine's brief depression is in recognition of the experience that must lie behind Frederic's worldly wisdom. But she is no coy mistress, and by her own will she overcomes her unhappiness and makes the best of their quarters and their farewell.

The action of book 3 centers on the retreat, and our modern Odysseus continues to survive calamities by exercising his wit and canniness. For instance, before Frederic and his drivers leave Gorizia, he orders the plan for servicing the vehicles and getting some sleep and food, and his men seem to respect his democratic leadership (189–93). Although his cleverness fails to extract his ambulances from the mud, he continues to lead his men until one is killed and another deserts. With only Piani left, he continues to figure out their retreat and indeed pulls it off. His escape from the battle police dramatically reveals his shrewdness under duress. From his brief observation of the conduct of the drumhead court-martial, he deduces his likely fate and acts boldly to avoid it (222–25). Then he exhibits survival skills that an Odysseus would admire, in dealing with both the elements (flooded river, bad weather) and man (battle police, train guards, the barman who runs an underground railroad for deserters [237–39]). In book 4 he is duplicitous with the friendly hospital porter and his wife, with his American friend Simmons, with his friend the barman in the hotel in Stresa, and finally in the outrageous but harmless and acceptable lies he tells the Swiss authorities: "You did not want something reasonable, you wanted something technical and then stuck to it without explanation" (281). And although one might find extenuation in context, he can also be deceitful with Catherine, not only early on in his game of romance, before he loves her, but also later.

When Emilio, the barman, comes to warn Frederic that he is about to be arrested, Frederic plays dumb even to his friend who is helping him. One might excuse his deceit of a friend if Frederic reasoned that Emilio would be culpable if he knowingly aided a deserter. Frederic had told him he was on convalescent leave and that he and Catherine were married (244–45). Now he tells Emilio he will take the extraordinary measure of rowing with his "wife" across a large stormy lake in November and across an international boundary at night because, merely, he doesn't "want to be arrested" (265). He never thinks of Emilio's possible trouble in providing a locked boat to a deserter (256). Like another runaway in a book Hemingway greatly admired, *Adventures of Huckleberry Finn,* Frederic Henry (his initials the reverse of Huck's) seems to dissemble, lie, and deceive not only for personal advantage and survival but also from force of habit. Of course, we assume that Emilio is smart enough to realize that Frederic is withholding the truth of his situation, and Emilio, beyond friendship as his motivation, believes Frederic will pay him handsomely for the rowboat if he succeeds in his escape. Curiously, as Frederic steps into the boat Emilio asks him if he paid for his hotel room. As an employee of a resort hotel, he might have some degree of loyalty to the anonymous, absent owner, but it seems an unusual question to ask in that moment of crisis. Frederic's assurance that he left money to pay for the room, however, reassures Emilio of Frederic's financial rectitude if not his honesty.

At exactly this point, Frederic deceives Catherine. Emilio had told Frederic that the storm was over: "it is rough but you will be all right" (265) and, later, "I don't think you'll get drowned" (269). In response to Frederic's thanks, he says in Italian, a language Catherine doesn't know, "You won't thank me if you get drowned." She then asks, "What does he say?" and Frederic lies, "He says good luck" (269). Again, one might understand Frederic's response in different ways. Why make Catherine worry or be upset? After all, Emilio had also said, "[Y]ou'll be all right." But Catherine has repeatedly proved herself as plucky and resourceful too. In the arduous escape, she helps as much as she can and provides a cheerful, even humorous spirit to buoy up Frederic. If Frederic knew the extent of her bravery and maturity, as he will in the tragic conclusion, he might not deny her an honest translation of Emilio's words. But honesty and openness are not part of his character. He is like Odysseus, Huck Finn, Holden Caulfield, and a host of other characters in picaresque adventures, a kind of hero who goes through life in disguises and who survives by dissembling, living by his wits, knowing more than he will let others, even his friends and loved ones, know.

Catherine's friend Helen Ferguson is the one character who in her Scottish rectitude reacts to this quality of Frederic—or, as she might put it, this lack of quality. Her motives might not be purely ethical, for Frederic has taken Catherine away from Helen and now when he returns from the battlefront promises to do so again, leaving Helen alone. In contrast to Catherine's joy and happy surprise at Frederic's return, Helen is first angry and then grief-stricken. She asks him why he is out of uniform, and his wisecrack answer, "I'm in the Cabinet," elicits not laughter from Helen but the intuitive accuracy of "You're in some mess," just as he had got Catherine pregnant in another "mess." Despite Catherine's exoneration of Frederic, Helen insists on his exclusive guilt as the dissembler that he has indeed revealed himself time and again to be. "He's done nothing but ruin you with his sneaking Italian tricks. Americans are worse than Italians," Helen indicts him, and later adds, "You're worse than sneaky. You're like a snake" (246).

After her bitter outburst, Helen calms down and admits to having been "unreasonable." But just as she had guessed right about Frederic being in trouble, she adumbrates Catherine's "ruin" at the end of the story. Before Catherine's death, Frederic uses his skills of deception once more to enable them to escape to Switzerland and be granted a comfortable internment there. Ironically, this final dissembling is filled with humor and seems to hurt no one (279–85). But the cleverness and craft that had so well served and saved him up to the end cannot help Catherine. Frederic is reduced to a helpless witness to her death and carries the painful knowledge that she dies precisely because he had set out to seduce her and had thus set in motion a chain of pitiless reactions.

The so-called Hemingway hero is by no means monolithic, one recurrent type merely with different names. Delbert Wylder's study of them quite sensibly denotes their plurality in his very title, *Hemingway's Heroes*. But just as one might expect a continuity in style and other elements of writing among an author's works, so one might be able to generalize cautiously that the stereotype of the Hemingway hero as an outgoing, courageous, virile man of action hardly suits most of his male protagonists. They may well be soldiers, boxers, big-game hunters, or deep-sea fishermen who lead violent lives or indulge in blood sports, but rather than being traditional heroes winning out over their adversaries, they frequently are victims or losers. They may seem to be strong and willful, but their stories often end in defeat, as Frederic and Catherine's does. They are the heroes to whom things happen, to whom things are done, *re*actors more than actors, even when their bodies and minds seem superior to those of ordinary creatures. They are modern humankind, buffeted by chance and controlled by the invisible strings of heredity and environment. Catherine's body, her inherited biology, betrays her. Frederic enters the war that, step by step, will lead to his entrapment.

His relationship with Catherine develops in the same aimless, unthinking way as he *reacts* rather than consciously planning and thinking about consequences—in short, acting maturely (if not heroically). He first learns of her presence from his friend and roommate, Lt. Rinaldi (in the third chapter), but evinces no curiosity or interest in her. Nor does he do so in the next chapter, when Rinaldi asks him to call on Catherine with him. To Frederic she is "very beautiful" (18), and her story of the death of her fiancé and Rinaldo's judgment at the end of their visit that Catherine prefers Frederic combine to encourage him to visit her again the next evening. At the first opportunity, he attempts to kiss her, and although she initially slaps him, she apologizes and then yields to his kiss and embrace. Apart from Catherine's behavior, Frederic's is clearly aggressive and self-indulgent. He will do and say anything, including "I love you" (30), to satisfy his desire, and it is only after his wounding that he believes he truly does love her.

Nevertheless, his actions in her regard continue to be spontaneous. Without any precaution or thought of consequences, he begins making love with her. Perhaps in this regard his actions are realistic, revealing him as a "mere mortal," flawed in character like most of us. But curiously, his actions are also heroic in the bold, uncalculating ways of the gods and demigods of myth. Zeus was continually indulging in amours with lovely mortals and "goddess[es]," as Rinaldo suggestively calls Catherine (66), without regard to the troubles such liaisons would create for him and others. Samson, Mark Antony, Othello, Joan of Arc, and countless other historical and literary characters share Frederic's flaw. That is, one of the most important qualities of Frederic's character is the tension in him between the impulses toward goodness and greatness (heroism) and those toward selfish satisfaction. Consider the many episodes in which food and drink play a role. In virtually every chapter Frederic and others eat and drink, and in the last chapter, when Catherine dies, Frederic leaves the hospital three times for a breakfast, a lunch, and a supper that are each described. (Obviously, eating, like much else in life, is routine, but when the author creates a narrator who attends repeatedly to any action, then we may assume a purposefulness to it. It is somehow organic to the story as, say, changing his socks is not.) At every chance, Frederic is also indulging his sexual appetite; however, the narrator is considerably reticent about the details of his lovemaking. These two animal drives are often seen as instincts to survival. But regardless of how the individual animal may be pleased or driven by them, the ultimate biological object of food and drink is for survival of the individual, whereas the ultimate biological object of sex is for survival of the species. Thus, Catherine's death in childbirth is seen by Frederic with bitter irony as "the by-product of good nights in Milan" (320). Perhaps this connection between life and death also motivates Catherine to say to him, the male whose touch brought her to this dismal end, "Don't touch me" (330) and then "It's just a dirty trick" (331). Although she uses the pronoun *it* in a vague way and in her gentility is unlikely to know the slang meaning of "dirty trick," it is indeed sex, *biology* (a word ironically meaning *the study of life*), that leads to her and her baby's death.

And Frederic, the would-be messiah in his recollection of the ants on the log of his campfire (327–28), has neither godlike nor heroic power to save Catherine. He is simply a witness to the death of strong and brave Catherine.

Elsewhere in the novel other episodes delineate this same flaw of the man who reacts more than acts, who has craft, but who repeatedly fails. He is the modern hero, nonheroic in that his strength of mind or body leads not to victory but to victimization. He may fight back, and at times he may appear to have won, but at last he and those closest to him lose. For two-thirds of the novel, Frederic is a good soldier, following orders and carrying out his duties as well as he can, albeit with a growing awareness of the futility of his actions and perhaps those of all the participants in the war. Even before his wounding, his thoughts and conversations with his drivers reveal his growing disillusionment (chapters 7 and 9). Even afterward the priest calls Frederic "a patriot" (71), someone committed to the national cause, and after his operation and recuperation Frederic returns to the front without hesitation, still the good soldier but with an ever-increasing sense of the madness around him. His conversation with the priest (chapter 26) reveals the change, as do his thoughts about patriotism in the key passage in which Frederic articulates (for himself only) his disillusionment (184–85). From having been called "a patriot" himself (71), he now diminishes Gino as "a patriot" and "a fine boy," that is, as naive and innocent. At this essential turning point, Frederic is still committed to his duty but no longer innocently so, as presumably he was on his enlistment. This development in his character intersects with a turning point in the war, as the Germans and Austrians successfully attack at a thinly defended point on the Italian front.

Still following orders, Frederic joins the retreat with his drivers and even undertakes to assist two sergeants and two sisters. The juxtaposition of the two episodes in which he shoots one of the sergeants for not obeying his order, followed late that night by the imminent shooting of *him,* just as summarily and arbitrarily, cannot but be the ironic watershed between the old Frederic and the new. He can and will no longer obey. He will not accept his meaningless death, and he makes his "separate peace" (243); the victim-rebel recognizes his failures, but because the ultimate act against him—his reasonless execution—would have been terminal, he rationalizes his decision not only to escape death but also to desert (232). Thus he is transformed, one might think, to an actor rather than a reactor, as he successfully escapes, makes his way back to Milan, assumes a civilian appearance, and tracks down Catherine. But after their successful escape to Switzerland, he reverts to his passive character, and the action of the concluding book 5 is governed not by anything Frederic does or says but by Catherine and the biological clock of her pregnant body. Apart from their lovemaking, Catherine had also initiated events earlier in their relationship. The episode at the racetrack is particularly revealing. The races (like the war, like one's biology) are fixed, and all they need do to win is find out from their friend Mr. Meyers what horse will win. But Catherine dislikes the ambience of their American and Italian acquaintances and persuades Frederic to leave them. She also persuades him to bet on a losing horse and then takes the initiative in ordering drinks and directing the conversation (131–32). It's a curious sequence, particularly considering the historical stereotype that the man in a couple will be the dominant figure, he the actor, she the passive reactor.

In the last four chapters, Frederic-Othello, "with his occupation gone"—as Catherine had quoted to him from *Othello* (257)—and with no more duty or obligation, is the remarkably passive one, not even thinking of his own or his family's future plans. Parts of five months pass by in book 5 while they await the birth of their child, but they *do* remarkably little. (Readers today should perhaps be reminded that for those pregnant women who could afford it, "lying in" was the period of confinement and inactivity preceding birth that modern gynecology no longer prescribes.) Frederic and Catherine's needs are largely taken care of by the *gut* (good) Guttingens, and their idyllic days are idle ones of leisurely meals and walks, much reading of books and magazines, and playing two-handed card games. The rather slow-moving, actionless last section of the novel further reduces an already-reactive Frederic to virtual passivity. Apart from the Guttingens, no other persons present are named in the section, not even the hairdresser who is "the only person we knew in Montreux" (292). After the perils of bombardment, retreat, and two escapes, Frederic's excitement consists of watching Catherine have her hair waved (292). When Catherine considerately suggests that he go off on a skiing trip for stimulation, he answers her questions with questions, and again at Catherine's suggestion he agrees to grow a beard. Out of context, the conversation borders on absurdity:

> "It might be fun. I'd like to see you with a beard."
> "All right. I'll grow one. I'll start now this minute. It's a good idea. It will give me something to do." (298)

Later in the same conversation Frederic teases Catherine: "And now do you want me to stop growing my beard or let it go on?" "Go on. Grow it. It will be exciting," she replies, using the same term Frederic had used, noting his excitement at her hairdressing (300).

In context, the conversation is part of the concluding section leading to a tragic denouement, and for all its static nature, it is nonetheless revealing. If fiction in its most basic terms is "character in action," here we have character revealed in virtual inaction. Frederic has no function other than through his loving presence to support Catherine. He lives vicariously through reading the newspapers and wondering how his old companions Rinaldo and the priest are faring in the war that goes "very badly" (292). Despite the idyllic setting and the couple's love for each other, Frederic repeatedly recalls the war and fails to willfully suppress thinking about it. Their togetherness and his "separate peace" are finally illusory, for they cannot live in a social vacuum. They are not Adam and Eve in a garden, for this Adam has brought a past with him; this Eve has brought a biological fate with her. They want to be a perfect and perfectly independent couple:

> "I want to be you too" [Catherine says].
> "You are. We're the same one" [Frederic replies]. (299)

And later they plan to express this desired unity by falling asleep at the same time. Frederic forebodes: "But we did not. I was awake for quite a long time thinking about things" (301). The purposeful ambiguity of his unidentified thoughts colors the entire idyll with the knowledge that it and their willed oneness are illusions. As much as they may desire solitude and each other, they cannot totally forsake the world of other "things."

Reactive rather than active, seeking pleasure for himself rather than others, and underhanded rather than honest are the nonheroic characteristics of the rogue. Frederic has been, as Ettore implies and as his conduct demonstrates, a "boozer and whorehound" (123), and both before and after he meets Catherine he has an eye for attractive women (84, 89, 135, 188). To his friend Rinaldi, Frederic's desire for Catherine makes him a "fool" (66); likewise, to the friendly nurse Miss Gage he is a "fool" (145). To his friend the priest, he is a deluded "patriot" in an unflattering sense (71). On occasion he brags (77, 104), flatters (109), and, as noted before, lies and deceives. He is sexually exploitive of Catherine (chapters 4–5) and insensitive to the fears of the two young sisters hitchhiking with his ambulance unit during the retreat (chapter 28). He can be sarcastic and mean, as in his description of the head nurse, Miss Van Campen, even when in an act of reconciliation she sends him an eggnog laced with sherry (86–88, 144). Although others (Catherine, Rinaldi, Dr. Valentini) often refer to him as a "boy," a "baby," and a "puppy" too, he patronizes his friend the priest by calling him "a fine boy" (72) and rather meanly describes people who befriend him. Ralph Simmons, the American singer of questionable vocal qualities, is sarcastically described as "always on the point of something very big happening. He was fat and looked shopworn around the nose and mouth as though he had hayfever" (120). Simmons is the man to whom Frederic later goes for aid after he has deserted, and Simmons generously helps him, giving him a suit of clothes that "were fine" (240–43). Are we to conclude that because Simmons has earlier been described as fat and Frederic later tells him "You're about my size" (242) that Frederic too is fat? More likely, Frederic's characterizations simply tend to be mean-spirited, as in his description of the hospital porter's wife, who has mended his clothes and who expresses great affection for him. She cries when he leaves the hospital, and he describes her as "a very short dumpy, happy-faced woman with white hair. When she cried her whole face went to pieces" (146). One might appreciate the keenness while also noting the unkindness of this not-unusual observation. Throughout the novel Frederic's rapier wit spares neither friend nor foe. Even Catherine receives a flippant response when, "upset and taut," she tells Frederic she is pregnant, and a response by him further disturbs her: "I could cut off my tongue," he facetiously replies (137–39).

Yet for all these negative characteristics, Frederic has other qualities that considerably complicate him, and we have only begun to understand him after realizing his deviation from conventional ideals of good behavior, let alone of heroic behavior. Indeed, it is because of his limitations that he is the necessary protagonist in this story. As in every story, character and action are inseparable parts of the unity of life. What we do is dependent on our character; our character is dependent on what we do. That evanescent idea of character shapes our lives; our character in turn is shaped by what happens to us in our lives.

Let us test a generalization about Frederic Henry by now focusing on his good qualities. At the beginning of his story he is an unshaped, unfinished entity, raw material, as it were, available for shaping and polishing. At the end of the story he is changed in important developmental ways. If he is self-centered, hedonistic, other- rather than inner-directed, worldly rather than philosophical and spiritual, nevertheless he seems to have potential for change and growth; even early on there are clues to this latent power of character. In the second chapter, he is the center of ribald and good-humored banter seemingly aimed at the priest but for his benefit as audience. He is given friendly advice, and the captain invites him to go with him to the bordello. In other words, Frederic, the outsider, is liked. In the next chapter, a strange but significant message is conveyed by Frederic's interaction with the young priest, and it begins a series of similar interactions with other characters, most notably Catherine, that suggest Frederic's inherent saving grace. His roommate, Rinaldi, who becomes a skilled surgeon in the war, also behaves affectionately toward Frederic, and they are "great friends" (12), as their behavior toward each other confirms.

The priest must have liked Frederic in a special way, for he had invited him to visit his family while on leave. Had the relationship been superficial, it is unlikely that the priest would then be "disappointed and suddenly hurt" that Frederic had not gone to his family's home in the pastoral Abruzzi region but had followed the ribald officers' advice. In the remarkably long and affective paragraph beginning "We two were talking," Frederic tries to explain to the priest what he had done on his leave, but he reaches a point where his words fail him: "I could not tell it" (13). The priest has not had the sensual experiences Frederic has, and those experiences mark a difference between them; nonetheless, "we were still friends" (14). And most important, Frederic reveals that if he has had experiences and a curiously ambiguous and inexpressible understanding as a result of them, the priest in his turn knows something Frederic doesn't: "He had always known what I did not know and what, when I learned it, I was always able to forget. But I did not know that then, although I learned it later" (14). Like the immediately preceding *it* that Frederic knew and the priest did not, this latter *it* is similarly ambiguous and tantalizing, arousing a curiosity that the reading of Frederic's whole story may finally satisfy. As Earl Rovit has noted in his *Ernest Hemingway*, Hemingway's characters can often be classified as tutors or tyros. Clearly here the priest, although inexperienced and young, is the potential teacher and Frederic his student. After Frederic's wounding, the priest visits him and they continue their discussion about their differences, the one tending to spirituality, the other to materiality, and again both repeatedly use an ambiguous *it*. But *it* is at least partly revealed as the love of God and a love that transcends lust (70–73).

On Catherine and Frederic's last night together in Milan, before he must return to the front, they will make love in the hotel room with the whorehouse decor, but right before that they stroll through the streets and to the great cathedral square. Although another soldier and "his girl" are embracing in the shadow of the cathedral, Catherine denies they are like Frederic and her. She also declines, at Frederic's invitation, to enter the cathedral. The gesture is a small one, indicating only a slight inclination to the *it* the priest knows. Surely it would be out of character in a realistic novel for Frederic to undergo a sudden spiritual conversion. But the scene is nonetheless appropriate, and part of a developing motif.

That some latent goodness lies below Frederic's surface self-centeredness is shown in the seventh chapter when he goes out of his way to help the ruptured soldier. That episode is also revealing of Frederic's ongoing willingness to treat rule and law loosely—a pragmatic characteristic that separates him from a culture of rigid right and wrong. His helping the soldier (a Good Samaritan deed by the side of a road) is a demonstration, an act of goodness, and not just the perception of potential for good that the priest and Catherine intuit in Frederic (33–36). He himself is aware that he has broken a code or rule in helping the malingering soldier. His own code of behavior gradually emerges as other adversities present themselves. From the unreflective "patriot" who so casually joins the army, to the person at the end who has completed his "education," Frederic changes in thought and deed. Casual as it may seem initially, this episode is the first to show Frederic's imminent growth.

This episode is followed (in the same chapter) by a passage about Frederic's thoughts on the war, and contrary to the priest's naming him a "patriot," his description of the war is most critical. If he had initially been an unthinking patriot, romantically believing with the Roman poet Horace and many latter-day patriots that "It is sweet and glorious to die for one's fatherland," he clearly no longer is such a person. He is not a hero like the "dreadful" and "conceited" Ettore (119–25) or the "patriot" Gino (184).

The transitions in the seventh chapter are suggestive: first the abortive Good Samaritan episode; next Frederic's critical reflections on the war, which he regards as personally harmless, like "war in the movies" (37); then his sexually exploitive thoughts about Catherine; then his drunken conviviality in the officers' mess; and finally his belated attempt to visit Catherine, who is ill and cannot see him. As his actions at the beginning of the chapter are his first efforts to do good, his thoughts at the end of the chapter are the first indications of his dawning morality. His behavior to this point had been amoral. Here he tries, unsuccessfully, to help a man, and he tries, unsuccessfully, to redeem his neglect of Catherine. For the first time in his account, he feels guilt, remorse: "I was feeling lonely and hollow" (41) are the last words of this transitional chapter.

The next step in his conversion to a more responsible, moral person occurs in the ninth chapter in which the first of two life-threatening events occurs. (The second is his impending drumhead trial and escape.) His severe wounding dramatically contradicts his recent thought that the war was harmless to him (37). Additionally, his earlier indifference to the war is eroded by the conversation with his four mechanic-drivers, led by the respectful and persuasive Passini, who concludes, "We will convert him" (48–51). The drivers' arguments are reflective of the actual historical growing awareness of the madness, cruelty, and immorality of war, and Frederic is receptive to their reasoning. "He likes it," Passini says, and then, in horrible proof of his argument, they are blown up by a huge trench mortar shell. All are wounded; Passini dies an agonized, agonizing death.

One might question the impact of this episode on Frederic's changing nature since he does not attempt to make his "separate peace," as his drivers were arguing that everyone should, until the second life-threatening event when he deserts. Between the two events, however, various episodes reveal the growing tension within Frederic. If his old Adam continues to be present in the confrontation with head nurse Van Campen (chapter 22) and that with the artillery captain on the train (chapter 24), that second confrontation ends with Frederic's concession that he was in the wrong. On the other hand, his conversation with the priest in the hospital (chapter 11) is not confrontational but defining of their differences. In it is the food for thought that continues from their earlier conversation (13–14). Curiously, the same tantalizing device of ambiguously using the pronoun *it* characterizes the second conversation too. Its use is realistic, no doubt, because they are discussing personal, delicate, and crucial thoughts and feelings on which they agree and disagree. The priest continues to be the tutor figure; Frederic, his reluctant student.

The priest is tired, perhaps emotionally exhausted by his hatred of the war. "I don't enjoy it," Frederic responds, with the *it* clearly referring to the war. But even though Frederic has been severely wounded, the priest disagrees, saying, "You do not mind it. You do not see it." Clearly there is a functional unclarity here as the priest-teacher contradicts Frederic. His first *it* could also refer to the war, but his second *it*—"You do not see it"—cannot. The priest continues in this way of speaking *around* some uncertainty: "Still even wounded you do not see it. I can tell. I do not see it myself but I feel it a little."

Then Frederic, apparently with some understanding of what the priest means but has not articulated, links their conversation with that of him and his men right before the explosion, the talk in which Passini was trying to "convert" Frederic: "When I was wounded we were talking about *it*. Passini was talking" (70; my emphasis). Again, more than the war is referred to by these *it*s. Beneath the surface appearances and actions of the war that maddens and destroys is another impulse to sanity and love. Even the conventional indications and appearances of class, rank, education, and money are misleading. In this important underlying way the priest recognizes that he is more like the enlisted men without power than like the officers. "It is not education or money [forms of power]. It is something else" that the priest "cannot say easily" when Frederic asks him to define the difference between them.

The priest's "lesson" is pessimistic as it pertains to the war and to the other struggle between those Italians who would wage peace and those who are blind to the madness and destruction of the war because the former are relatively powerless. But despite his gloomy thinking about the war, some other *it* makes the priest "suddenly very happy." That *it* is the Abruzzi region, his Edenic homeland: "Yes, I love it very much" (71). Then the essential difference between them (and at least the partial answer to the ambiguous *it* ending chapter 3) is revealed in the priest's catechism as love, either the love of God or the love of one's fellow human beings. Interestingly, Frederic does not claim to be godless; he claims only to not love God. (He does say he fears God sometimes.) Nor does he love anyone. But the priest three times contradicts him; the priest has perceived in Frederic some potential for a love that is not selfish, that will make him happy in a way he has never known. That transcendent love is the referent of the ambiguous *it,* whether a love of God or of fellow human beings.

This serious and honest conversation contrasts with those earlier "wineful" ones of chapters 2 and 3 that both ended with Frederic getting up and leaving (and at least once going to the whorehouse). Here it is the priest who will leave Frederic, but not before Frederic balances the priest's three contradictions with three requests to extend their discussion ("Don't go. . . . [T]alk. . . . Come and see me again" [72–73]). In his "education," this chapter tells an important lesson.

The profane Frederic is now ready for a transition in the hands of another tutor, Catherine. It is remarkable that in neither his talk nor his thoughts in chapter 11 does Catherine appear. After the priest leaves, Frederic has a reverie not of her but of the priest's beloved Abruzzi. Indeed, Catherine is absent from the novel for five chapters, and she is present in Frederic's thought very rarely and definitely not as someone beloved.

After Frederic's wounding, Rinaldi visits him in the field hospital, and Frederic thinks to ask about Catherine only after Rinaldi reminds him of the presence of "the English" (64). Twice Rinaldi says he will bring Catherine to see Frederic, and thrice he says he will send her, but for some unexplained reason she never comes. In any case, after Rinaldi offers to go bring Catherine, Frederic's response seems to indicate a lack of ardor for her. He tells Rinaldi to stay and asks him about the whorehouse girls, not about Catherine. Of course, such a change of subject might be evidence of Frederic's wiliness. Temporarily unable to continue his affair with Catherine, he may not wish to have Rinaldi take advantage of his wounding. But Rinaldi seems to have no such inclination, as he offers repeatedly to bring or send her and then describes her contemptuously as a "lovely cool goddess," fit only for worship (66). Without knowing of the priest's following conversation, Rinaldi nevertheless foreshadows their talk of the worship of God. Rinaldi later returns to tell Frederic that, like him, Catherine will be transferred to a hospital in Milan. Even then Frederic evinces no thought of or desire for Catherine, and on arrival at the hospital in Milan his eye is for Miss Gage, the "young and pretty" nurse. Further, when he asks if Catherine is at the hospital and is told she is not, he continues to exclude her from his thoughts.

An ardent lover he is not, but a remarkable transformation then occurs. As if to clear the record, Frederic repays the kindness of Miss Gage with patronizing remarks and the otherwise-gratuitous judgment that in "bright sunlight" "she looked a little older . . . and not so pretty" (89). Besides further demonstrating this ungenerous-if-not-mean-spirited flaw in Frederic's character, the judgment establishes that when Catherine shortly appears—conveniently if not miraculously plucked from the hospital in Gorizia and deposited in one in Milan, more than 200 miles away—she will have no rival and her Don Juan will have no embarrassing flirtation with Miss Gage to explain. His reaction to Catherine's arrival and her reaction to his sudden ardor may strain our credulity: "When I saw her I was in love with her" (91). The simplicity of the statement pivots rhythmically on the clause "I was." Its directness and the context of the episode—in which Frederic totally avoids his customary ironic, sarcastic, and other defensive postures—may persuade us of his honesty. That the lovers, one in a nurse's uniform and the other swathed in bandages, should then make love in broad daylight in his hospital bed is no less credulous than Frederic's sudden affirmation of love.

To Catherine, the sexual act is confirmation of her love for Frederic: "Now do you believe I love you?" she asks him (92). But she also repeatedly asks for confirmation of his love for her, for she knows he has had a different (a male? a dual?) standard for lovemaking: "You do love me? . . . You really love me? . . . You do love me, don't you?" she asks, both before and after their lovemaking. We might well be as dubious as she were it not for the prior episodes with the priest, who (like Friar Laurence in *Romeo and Juliet*) has acted as a go-between for the lovers. For all his previously demonstrated flaws, Frederic's potential is here realized in a sudden but plausible transformation. The hardheaded, ironic, selfish Frederic is not miraculously changed, but he is changed: "God knows I had not wanted to fall in love with her. I had not wanted to fall in love with any one. But God knows I had" (93).

Just as the priest had intuited a basic goodness within Frederic, so too had Catherine, and from this point Frederic's growth will come largely at her hands. The priest, Frederic's drivers, Count Greffi, and Frederic's own observations will likewise be instrumental in his continuing education, but Catherine now is the principal, and it is to her character that we now turn.

Catherine Barkley

If Frederic Henry is not traditionally heroic, one might expect Catherine Barkley, his mate, to share his nature and values. Yet there are many important differences between them. Just as Frederic had been attracted to the priest despite their great differences, so it seems with Frederic and Catherine. But the very presentation of her character is also different, and she poses a challenge to our understanding. Indeed, surveying the critical literature that touches on her reveals a bewildering variety of responses. At the one extreme she is perceived as a one-dimensional pasteboard figure, a mere passive sexual object, without thoughts and feelings of her own, the dream-girl stereotype of male chauvinists: young, beautiful, sexually pliant, an attractive adornment in public places (hotels, restaurants, racetracks), a socially required extension of an egotistic male and guaranteed for trouble-free performance to middle age, when, beginning to show her mileage, she can be traded in by the male for the latest model, someone with racier lines if not a bucket seat. Thus baldly put, one might so judge Catherine, varying the analogy only slightly to require an early trade-in because of the manufacturer's biological mistakes. And so she has been seen by some readers, from the earliest reviewers on and including the usually astute Edmund Wilson. He needed no feminist movement to judge Hemingway's women characters as underdeveloped.[14]

At the other extreme (a position less well represented in the criticism), Catherine may be perceived as a fully developed character, realistic, important in her own right, and as much an actor in the drama as Frederic is. Rather than unheroic like Frederic, she could also be perceived as a heroine in the romantic rather than the realistic tradition of fiction: courageous (both morally and physically), strong of mind and body, bold, noble, and a protector of and sacrificer for others. These interpretations can also be supported by particular emphases in one's reading, but that is not to make of Catherine a chimera who can be whatever any particular reader says she is.

Much of the joy of reading is continual discovery within a triangular relationship. At the base of the triangle we can imagine a text, in this case *A Farewell to Arms*. The other sides of the figure are the author, here Ernest Hemingway, and we the readers, possibly infinite in number.

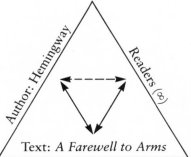

Hemingway created the novel (thus the arrow to it), but the novel in turn affected him both in the complex writing process and afterward. (Thus the arrow points both ways.) Similarly, diverse readers go to the novel, and it in turn comes to them. Indirectly, then, Hemingway and his readers interact (thus the broken arrow). One might expect the source of the variations in interpretation to be the readers, with their wide-ranging differences in experience, intelligence, attentiveness, and preconceptions, but neither the novel itself nor certainly its author is fixed and invariable. Great works of art tend to exist over time within a changing world of people and perceptions, and this larger reality needs also to be considered. It is a universal context of unimaginable scope, but as this diagram suggests, we can imagine much of it.

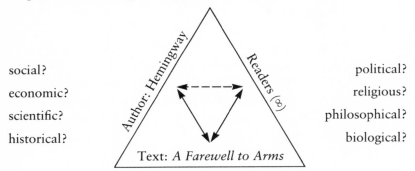

We feel this larger reality even when we do not know it, and with a certain audacity and self-confidence we live in this world we know so little of. We live in it poorly or well, and vicariously through the novel our limited lives are given variety and experience. If even the simplest tales, such as a nursery rhyme or a biblical parable, evince multiple responses, how much more challenging must be an intricately woven novel and one of its major characters?

All this is by way of returning to the enigmatic Catherine and with degrees of both humility and adventure trying to comprehend her. Understanding Catherine requires a radical shift from the way we approach Frederic's character because he is the narrator as well as the protagonist. Obviously, had Hemingway chosen to make Catherine the protagonist or had he chosen an objective point of view from which to tell the story—such as the omniscient, in which the narrator is godlike and can see and know all, including the thoughts of all characters—the story would be considerably different. As we have it, however, the understanding of the narrator, Frederic, is finite, and no matter how shrewd, clever, and experienced he is, he does not know all. Moreover, his tendency toward egotism further limits his capacity to portray Catherine. But as he shows us his character evolving, he grows into a more gentle, less egotistic person, one who becomes more attentive to Catherine as an individual in her own right. In any case, assuming that Frederic reports his speech and actions accurately, we can judge and understand her on that record, however limited. Thus, if she is perceived as a stereotypical male chauvinist's dream-girl, it is because that is how Frederic initially perceives her: "Miss Barkley was quite tall. She wore what seemed to be a nurse's uniform, was blonde and had a tawny skin and gray eyes. I thought she was very beautiful" (18). Their initial conversation (18–20) then turns to her fiancé, killed the previous year, and in their talk Frederic shrewdly learns Catherine's feelings of guilt for not having married the man or given him "it" (that magical word): "He could have had it all," she says. Frederic flatters her, tells her he has never loved anyone, and contradicts her when she says her fiancé's death "was the end of it." What a peculiar response he makes: "I don't know." It doesn't suggest that Frederic believes in an afterlife; rather, it indicates that he is hoping he will get some of *it,* especially since Catherine feels guilty about once before having preserved her virginity. Her insistence that she is right—"Oh, yes. . . . That's the end of it"—reveals that she has not caught Frederic's meaning.

One might infer from this initial conversation that Catherine is articulate, that she has suffered a trauma from which she is recovering and from which she thinks she has learned, and that she is remarkably open as she talks to a new acquaintance about her intimate life. Further, she is not passive in her talk, as she, like Frederic, asks questions and makes judgments, such as telling him she thinks it "an odd thing—to be in the Italian army." She also politely contradicts Frederic's view that "There isn't always an explanation for everything," and when he makes a patronizing response, "That's awfully nice," she again politely but firmly challenges him:

> "*Do* we have to go on and talk this way?"
> "No," I said.
> "That's a relief. Isn't it?" (18)

Later she continues to hold her own in the conversation when it turns to the war. In a male-dominated society, war is a male topic as well as a male pursuit. Certainly in the first half of this century, women were supposed to know about cooking and children, and they were accepted in female-dominated professions, such as public school teaching and nursing. But Catherine has a hard view of the war, one learned through bitter experience. She will not demurely avoid the subject of the war they are in, and she has strong opinions about it and here gets in the last word. She will not be lectured by or defer to Frederic simply because he is male. She does not say so; nor does Frederic reflect on her polite assertiveness. The episode demonstrates her character, and neither Catherine nor Frederic reflects on her behavior as being unusual or surprising. Thus, embedded in the dialogue and much more persuasive than any stereotypical and unfounded judgment is the beginning of the revelation of Catherine's character to both Frederic and the reader. Such scene-by-scene attentiveness to what Catherine actually says and does, as reported by Frederic and in our awareness of his motives, is more reliable than inferences based on generalizations about the character of beautiful young Scottish nurse's aides in Italy during World War I. One suspects that much of the debate on Catherine's true nature (and Hemingway's ability to present her) would be resolved by making inferences based on her speech and actions, rather than on generalizations about women to whom she relates in superficial ways. (Other stereotypes are also at issue, such as the sexual promiscuity that supposedly increases during wartime. Apropos that point, Frederic does not report or even allude to any such behavior among the other nurses or any other women, except for the prostitutes, whose profession it is. The two young sisters of chapters 28–29 are clearly not interested in random sex but instead fear it.)

In the next episode, Frederic makes his pass at Catherine, who at first rebuffs him with a hard slap and then apologizes, not for rebuffing him but for hurting him by her reaction. As the sly, sexually experienced Frederic plots his moves, he makes up an excuse for his behavior and also flatters her: " 'You see I've been leading sort of a funny life. And I never even talk English. And then you are so very beautiful.' I looked at her" (26). What a masterstroke! He looks at her *after* he says she is "so very beautiful." Both his timing and his "lines" are worthy of a sentimental romance, grade B, and Catherine sees through it: "You don't need to say a lot of nonsense," for nonsense it is, as if his "funny life" were any different from all others in the uprooting of war. However comforting it may be to speak one's native language, the rationalization of not doing so as an excuse for Frederic's sexual advance is an absurdity of a different sort, but it is still "nonsense," and Catherine here reveals her astuteness.

She then reveals her own warmth and attraction to Frederic by offering to kiss him, and he takes the opportunity to extend her offered kiss of friendship into a deep sexual kiss and embrace that Catherine first resists and then emotionally yields to. Astute in her prior reaction, she is clearly tricked and vulnerable here. She is the antithesis of Frederic in his pursuit of the sexual "it." The *it* she wants is the kind of love the priest believes in, spiritual and total commitment and not merely carnal love.

Her next meeting with Frederic again reveals both her astuteness and her vulnerability and also introduces an explanation for the latter, her "madness" or imbalance, partly as a result of the death of her fiancé. Having been away on ambulance duty, Frederic returns to see her three days after their second meeting. One might think her initial behavior is more apt for a woman in a long-term relationship with a man as she inquires where he has been and why he hadn't sent her a note. Although earlier she addressed him formally—"Mr. Henry"—within earshot of the hospital orderly, she now calls him "darling" as they stroll in the garden and she gently admonishes him: "You ought to have let me know, darling. . . . You've been away a long time" (30). And then, in an exchange that leads Frederic to conclude that "she was probably a little crazy," she continues to be the director, the controller, the dominant or leading partner in their intimate love. Although Frederic is clearly the protagonist and the leader apart from Catherine, the man who is acted on by many forces outside his control (the army, the enemy, the weather, chance) is also acted on by Catherine, who in some ways is a stronger character than he.

In this scene she, the "crazy" one, manipulates the rational Frederic in order to relieve her grief, to substitute Frederic for her lost fiancé, but at the end of it, she returns to reality, having played *her* game while Frederic thinks he is playing *his* game, moving toward seduction. As she had first directed him "We *have to* just walk here" (my emphasis), she then extracts his false admission of love, and tells him what to say, the words she has long known her dead fiancé will never say—"I've come back to Catherine in the night"—and she in turn avows her love for Frederic, transferring to him, in psychoanalytical terms, her feelings for her lost fiancé (30). Frederic's object of gratification is here juxtaposed with his alternative of the whorehouse, in which the game of love is professional, that is, for money. The exchange Catherine wills is for the restoration of a love that is transcendent, restorative, and fulfilling of her own capacity to love another being. Frederic is frustrated in his desire because there is no private place where they can go to make love, but Catherine had gone off, metaphorically, in her game: "She came back from wherever she had been" (31). The shift suggests the advantage Catherine has of transference in the game of love for her own relief, however temporary. In the next moment she can return to reality, ending the "rotten game" and acknowledging it in the face of Frederic's pretended ignorance (31).

Although Frederic wanted to continue the game, it is Catherine who ends it and Catherine who pronounces him an incomplete success as a surrogate for her dead lover. Frederic doesn't even pronounce "Dear Catherine" as the fiancé did, and she further suggests his failure in comparison with her fiancé by adding, "But you're very nice. You're a very good boy" (31). Her intuition (like the priest's awareness) is of Frederic's basic goodness, but at the same time her observations are somewhat patronizing. She knows what Frederic is after, she calls him a *boy,* and she presents the terms of their future relationship: he will come and see her as a friend. She offers a handshake, yields to Frederic's request for a kiss, and breaks away from it to leave him. Her victory is confirmed not by a single word of what he says or thinks but by what he does and what he records Rinaldi saying to him. Even though the revelry at the bordello continues, he passes it up and goes to his room. His friend Rinaldi observes that "Baby [compare *boy*] is puzzled"—the result of "Calling on the British." Is not the worldly and sensitive Rinaldi's reply an indication of Catherine's having bested Frederic in the game of love? "Thank God I did not become involved with the British" (32). The stakes in the game of love are higher than the innocent boy-baby Frederic, for all his sexual experience and worldly knowledge, is aware. Confirmation of his gentle entrapment follows at the end of the next chapter, when he remembers his date with Catherine. But she is ill and cannot see him. In a relatively mild way her body has betrayed her, as it will again mortally at the end of the story. At this earlier point, Catherine "wins" again in the love match as Frederic feels remorse and "lonely and empty . . . lonely and hollow" for having taken "Catherine very lightly" (41).

Catherine sees him off to the front the following morning, and again in their brief conversation she controls and directs, telling him to come see her on his return, not to say "good-by," to be good and careful, and not to kiss her there in public. Frederic obeys. But (as noted before) Catherine disappears from the story by virtue of the plot's then focusing on Frederic's wounding and its aftermath. A similar rhythm occurs when Frederic returns to the front and the necessity of the plot leaves Catherine in Milan. Thus she is absent from chapters 9–13 and 25–33. (She is also absent from 4 of the first 8 chapters and from chapter 22—thus from 19 of the total of 41.)

When they are reunited in the hospital in Milan, Frederic is suddenly aware that he is in love with Catherine, and if earlier it was she who was "crazy" in her grief and confounding of Frederic and her dead fiancé, a change now occurs. Catherine gives in to his insistent pleas to make love, but only after Frederic repeatedly avows his true love. Although the scene of a uniformed nurse's aide making love to a bedridden, badly wounded soldier may put some strain on our credulity or tease our imagination, Catherine's character further emerges as the one in control. It is Frederic who is "crazy about her," and it is she who in an ancient ceremony seals their mutual love in sexual consummation. "Now do you believe I love you?" may be so common as to be a funny cliché, but in context (and "in character") it seems right—honest and fitting (92). If in their lovemaking Frederic is the more ardent partner, it is Catherine who uses it to ensnare Frederic, again in an old human rite, but no more invalid (or less human) for its commonness.

Entrapment, of course, is a loaded term, with associations that are male, not female. If Frederic "had not wanted to fall in love with her" (93), he does not regret having done so, and if Catherine is indeed a fine woman, he is at worst in a tender trap and at least in an unselfish love in which she as his tutor will teach him much about life and death.

Is she a credible character? Does the question not suggest that to the degree that she—or anyone—approaches an ideal, she is less credible because she is less like the average person? And paired with Frederic, who less well approaches an ideal, would the beautiful, kind, attentive, intelligent Catherine use those qualities to ensnare *or* elevate a much lesser creature? Answers perhaps cannot be categorical, but they will depend not solely on depictions of Catherine—for she is seen and presented only by Frederic—but on the interactions between him and her. Even though it is his story to tell, we can trust the story more than him. A good example of their interaction occurs in chapter 16. Except for the first paragraph and five short sentences, the episode consists of an extensive dialogue between them. It is indeed a stylistic tour de force, one resembling a scene in a play in which the playwright provides introductory information to "set the stage" and then, except for the four narrative sentences (like "She kissed me"), the two "actors" exchange lines. In some parts of his other novels and in such short stories as "The Killers" and "Hills Like White Elephants" Hemingway also used this dramatic or scenic style. In an actual play, the director and actors then interpret the lines, sometimes with short indications from the playwright as to how they are to be presented: The King [sarcastically]: Kissed me?

Here, with one important exception, the lines are marked only with the conventional tags of "she said," "Catherine said," and "I said," and often even they are absent in the stichomythic dialogue. The exception, in contrast, leaps off the page to remind us of Frederic's predisposition to deceit: " 'No,' I lied" (105). It is in response to Catherine's question asking him whether he'd ever told a prostitute that he loved her. In one sense, it is a white lie of little matter, since Frederic has already informed us that he has never been in love. In effect, then, he is lying about a lie, having lied to at least one prostitute that he loved her (or them) for whatever reason but presumably to gain some advantage or favor. In other words, because he was lying to a prostitute it is therefore all right to lie to Catherine in order to "correct" the record, rather than explaining at some length, "Yes, I have told prostitutes I loved them but not in the way or with the intention you mean." Even when Catherine is saying, "Tell me the truth," assuring him that she can take it without offense or harm, he lies. She is convinced, and her response, "I knew you wouldn't," is followed by "Oh, I love you, darling" (105).

Earlier in this conversation she had forced Frederic to admit he was lying when he said he had never "stayed with" a woman. Yet she doggedly pursues her questioning, playing a game in which Frederic tells lies that she knows are lies to determine if he had ever loved anyone else. When Frederic does tell the truth, he does so in the third person, following Catherine's lead and thus not implicating himself: when Catherine asks, "Does *she* [the prostitute] say she loves him?" Frederic responds, "Yes. If *he* wants her to"—not "If *I* want her to" (my emphasis). Then when he (apparently) successfully lies to her, saying that *he* never told a whore he loved her, Catherine's pleased reaction is to assure Frederic that she will say and do whatever he wants, losing herself in him, as she then placidly demonstrates when he orders her to "come to bed again" (106).

It would be enlightening, I think, to have trained, sensitive actors perform the roles of Frederic and Catherine in the "play." In gesture, intonation, timing, and movement they might discover what is inherent in but also buried in the scene and its lines. At one point Catherine first asserts an opinion different from Frederic's: "I didn't like him [Dr. Valentini] as much as you did." She next denies Frederic's plea to return to bed. She then contradicts him in her greater knowledge of postoperative behavior, again denies his order to return to bed, and diverts his selfish and childish "You don't really love me or you'd come back again" by calling him the "silly boy" that he is and by going about her nursing duties, including cleaning him inside and out. Two pages of the dialogue occur while she is giving him an enema and casually talking of her proprietary concern for his care, concern about her possible transfer, and concern that he might reveal their intimacy under anesthesia. In other words, she is remarkably cool, efficient, and professional, as well as continuing to show that she more than Frederic is in control of their behavior. Her talk is also "cool," and she reveals herself to be the more pragmatic of the two, even though she also recognizes how her intense love of Frederic can make her "silly" in her possessiveness, not wanting the other nurses and aides to touch him (103).

Her talk is loving but edged with irony and wit, as in "You've such a lovely temperature. . . . I'm awfully proud of your temperature" and in the funny non sequitur in reply to Frederic's "Valentini will fix me": "He should with those mustaches" (103). All through this scene Frederic has one overriding purpose, whether by imprecation or deceit—to persuade Catherine to make love to him. But she will yield to him only after she has fulfilled her duties and also has dominated the conversation and extracted from Frederic some knowledge of his past love life. That on one important question she does not know he is lying in no way detracts from her character. At that very point he curiously interrupts their dialogue with two of the five sentences (beyond the first paragraph of the chapter) that are not dialogue. He has just successfully lied and Catherine has intently avowed her love in what must be, at least partly, a cause-effect sequence. But then comes the short interruption before the dialogue is resumed: "Outside the sun was up over the roofs and I could see the points of the cathedral with the sunlight on them. I was clean inside and outside and waiting for the doctor" (105).

Surely the close juxtaposition of the imagery of the sun, roofs, and spires of the cathedral (Apollonian in their suggestions), the *outsides* that link the first with the second sentence, and its reference to Catherine's giving him a bath and an enema are wonderfully ironic. The lying-in-bed liar is not "clean" the way Catherine is, but his deceit has made her look at him "very happily" (105). If Frederic then achieves his wish of having her return to bed with him, she achieves a selfless goodness, willing to serve him sexually even when she deprecatingly says, "I'm afraid I'm not very good at it yet" (106). She is good at everything else: her professional duties, her wit, and her love. If her interrogation of Frederic's past love life suggests her insecurity, her motive is to allay those feelings and to cement the bond between them. If she is being honest and self-aware, there is something pathetic about her saying, "There isn't any me any more. Just what you want" (106). But in fact she has not in this episode submerged, nor does she subsequently totally submerge her selfhood or have no desire of her own or capacity for independent action. Although her prevailing desire is to love and be loved, such close reading as of this episode and others reveals a complex, multifaceted person. If her desire is for an ultimately unachievable ideal love, she also aspires to ideal personhood. One cannot be good for someone else without also being good for oneself. Frederic notes the reciprocity simply and directly: "I loved her very much and she loved me" (108).

Thus we must treat her statements of abnegation and absorption of her self in Frederic as a sincere ideal aspired to but practically impossible. In the last chapters of the novel, she continues to express such ideas as "I want you so much I want to be you too" (299). But as we test Frederic's character by what he does as well as says, so too does Catherine emerge as a rounded character apart from her idealistic statements. Indeed, if they are understood as a kind of lover's propaganda, sincere but nonetheless meant to have a persuasive effect, she is successful, for Frederic himself begins to voice a similar ideal that is unsupported by the action. Just as earlier he had subscribed to the priest's vision of the Edenic Abruzzi but instead had gone to the cafés and whorehouses, here later in the novel both lovers recognize an ideal but learn to live within the real world. In Stresa, when they are separated for two hours while Catherine is visiting her friend Ferguson, Frederic reads the newspapers, chats with the barman, and goes fishing with him. Never in this sequence is his mood revealed, except that he tells the barman that the war is "Rotten" and he "was a fool" for going to war (255–56). But clearly he does not afterward feel good while he is waiting alone for Catherine. And "When Catherine came back it was all right again" (256). Fishing, billiards, and reading may be done with some satisfaction apart from Catherine, but here he at least *says* pretty much what she had said and what she manipulates him into repeating:

> "All you have is me and I go away."
> "That's true. . . ."
> "Now if you aren't with me I haven't a thing in the world. . . ."
> "I'm just so in love with you that there isn't anything else."
> (257)

These remarks in other contexts (such as Frederic's returning to the war from the hospital) could easily be read and understood with him making the first statement and Catherine the other three. But now Catherine has brought him around to echo her earlier speech and her continuing actions. On the one hand is the expressible ideal of love; on the other, the inexpressible realization of it.

Chapter 20 provides another good indication of Catherine's strength of character and leadership. It's a curious chapter in a novel of love and war. It may at first seem hardly crucial, dispensable even, and most commentaries on the novel ignore it. But if one is interested in Catherine's character, it is one of the few early chapters in which she is present with Frederic in an extended episode. The narration is straightforward and unsurprising in its presentation of a conventional recreational activity of going to the races. Frederic is, by and large, merely an observer of the scene. For their first bet, Catherine's certainty that one horse was dyed leads all four in the group to bet on it. They win but other bettors, also aware of the fix, have driven down the odds, and Catherine's and her group's winnings are greatly reduced. Catherine's reaction is again funny: "Then we won't get three thousand lire. . . . I don't like this crooked racing!" (129).

Although the attributions of the next two lines of dialogue are unstated, presumably the speakers are Frederic and Catherine, the former matter-of-fact ("We'll get two hundred lire") and the latter indignant and assertive ("That's nothing. That doesn't do us any good. I thought we were going to get three thousand"). When Ferguson echoes Catherine's somewhat-hypocritical but amusing judgment about crooked racing, Catherine perceives and acknowledges the irony for the group, and when they are joined by two Italians and the vice-consul McAdams, the latter "talked to Catherine" (130). These details are subtle indications of her social control, awareness, and leadership.

The episode continues in this vein. Frederic bets again on a tip from "Old Meyers," who is involved in the crooked racing, and does not even know the horse's name. Catherine wryly observes, "You have touching faith" (131). Such words cannot come from a pasteboard character, and she, not the passive Frederic, controls what they do (albeit in a gentle way). She is annoyed by the crooked, mirthless Meyers, who, in further comedy, is angered that so many bettors are in on the fix but ironically refuses to let his own wife in on the information, and Catherine is annoyed by the equally amusing, overly mannered Italians. That is, Frederic sees them differently from how Catherine does, and she *tells* Frederic, "I'll go down with you . . . to the paddock" (131), and also gently disagrees with Frederic about his liking and her disliking their racetrack companions. To further the comedic business about the fixed racing, she even persuades Frederic to bet on a losing horse in order for *her* to "feel so much cleaner" (131). Perhaps Frederic is having a little sexist joke at Catherine's expense. Frederic has "touching faith," but it's faith in a virtually sure thing, a fixed race, whereas Catherine feels "cleaner" when they *lose* their bet. That's a woman for you (a sexist might say), preferring to lose, just like dopey Mrs. Meyers, who could win merely by asking her husband. Yet Catherine's behavior is a rejection of immorality, and her taking Frederic away from the scene of "fixed" manners as well as fixed racing is a sign of her superior nature. If the war is "fixed" and love is "fixed" and all is "fixed," she will yet act *as if* the world were not so. She will not "cheat."

The episode concludes with considerable ironic tension between Catherine's resistance to the artificial and Frederic's passive acceptance of it. He had told Catherine he liked the ambience, but she takes him away from it, however briefly, and she takes the lead in ordering drinks, preventing Frederic from going to get them. And in putting up her hand she subverts every Emily Post code of ladylike behavior. It's a "masculine" act. Her conversation is "feminine" when she puts her opinion in the form of a question; that is one of the nonassertive ways of women and servants: "Don't you like it better when we're alone?" rather than "It's better when we're alone" or somesuch. And Frederic dutifully replies, "Yes."

But Catherine is not only assertive. She is also carefully attuned to Frederic's different feelings. He attempts to mask them by agreeing with Catherine and passively noting another of her "feminine" paradoxes— "I felt very lonely when they were all there." Catherine appreciates his behavior even as she sensitively sees through his polite sacrifice and offers her own in return. The last paragraph is heavily sardonic, as Frederic notes the hollow triumph of his passive position over Catherine's gently moral one: "After we had been alone awhile we were glad to see the others again. We had a good time" (132). Did Catherine? We cannot know, but we can ask the question.

Throughout the novel Catherine's speech and actions are always limited to those observable by Frederic, the narrator, and he might well filter them through a prejudicial consciousness, tending at least to remember her favorably. But if he frankly reveals that he is deceitful with Catherine and others, his very manner of sardonically telling his story is assurance that his remarks about Catherine are as accurate as he can make them. Some illustrations of them indicate that she is

- dutiful, coming to see him only after performing her nursing duties (136);
- philosophical, placing her problems in perspective (135); and

- very loving, but in her love knowing she cannot lose her own ego, as shown when she challenges Frederic—" 'Always' isn't a pretty word" (139)—and *prods* him when he makes a little joke about himself that she disagrees with (140).

One's attention to Catherine's actions and speech, to Frederic's *reaction* to her, to Helen Ferguson's being "very good to" her (108), and to others' attention and kindness to her leaves us with only Rinaldi's dissent about her, offered to Frederic in both worldly wisdom and friendly envy when Frederic returns from an early date with Catherine— "Thank God I did not become involved with the British" (32)—and that too is a statement that in a sense is flattering of Catherine. To become "involved" with an ordinary woman would presage a casual affair, the kind of flirtation Rinaldi would enjoy apart from his surgeon's duties. But as he later describes Catherine as "Your lovely cool goddess" (66), his exaggeration suggests her special qualities. She is not a person to be taken lightly. No goddess, she treds the ground; she is fallible, human, strongly frail even as she is intelligent and kind. Or so the story says.

She also takes over that story in the concluding book 5, in which her and Frederic's actions focus on her pregnancy. Indeed, the two *do* very little except live together in virtual isolation, awaiting the baby. The description Frederic gives of their life in a mountainside chalet sounds idyllic, and Catherine seems contented and happy. She continues to be the gentle leader of the two, and not only because of the necessities of her biology. It is she who chooses to "have beer instead of tea," though the bibulous Frederic is hardly likely to argue the choice (293). It is she who brings up the subject of marriage and yet rejects Frederic's willingness to marry immediately (293). She also has pragmatically looked up the American law of legitimacy and tells the American Frederic what that law is, as well as the places in America she wishes to visit. That is, without asking Frederic's opinions or desires she makes assumptions about their future to which he acquiesces, just as she decides for the immediate time when they will return to their chalet from their visit to Montreux (295).

One other curious assumption of hers concerns the sex of the baby. Catherine believes the baby is female and refers to it as "young Catherine," as if the baby were, or were to become, a female extension of herself. There may be many reasons for wanting a baby of a particular sex, but in the patriarchal world of this novel, Catherine's assumption suggests a divergence, an independence, an assertiveness all in keeping with her gentle strength throughout the story. On the other hand, Frederic might be assumed to share in the general cultural mores of a patriarchy in which fathers desire sons before daughters. Indeed, in the extreme forms, wives who could not "produce" male heirs were considered deficient and could be divorced or "set aside." Frederic's only resistance to Catherine's assumption is mild and humorous but nonetheless telling. If Catherine succeeds in keeping "her small enough and she's a boy, maybe he will be a jockey" (293). The response to Catherine's assumption might be understood as a concession with a rider: "Yes, I'll let you decide and lead, as I often do, but I'll have my little sardonic joke that acknowledges that the female is superior to the male, that a male baby would be metaphorically as well as literally a smaller version of a female." Catherine disdains to acknowledge Frederic's joke and changes the subject. Nor can Frederic have the last laugh, for as he recalls and records this exchange, he knows Catherine was wrong; the baby is a boy. At his birth, the nurse (presumably a woman) participates in the general cultural assumption that men desire male children: "Aren't you proud of your son? . . . Didn't you want a boy?" But to both questions, Frederic flatly answers, "No" (325). The male baby is dead, and he has in a sense killed his mother.

Earlier in the novel Catherine often displays a strength of character that contrasts with Frederic's and that he perceives and admires. When they are rowing across the lake to refuge in Switzerland, she has that "grace under pressure" that was, to Hemingway, the essence of courage. Although Frederic does most of the rowing and is good at it, Catherine takes a turn to let him rest and is otherwise helpful, not the least in her cheerfulness and good humor. She also has the idea to use the umbrella as a sail, and when Frederic is miffed by her laughter at him, she jollies him and characterizes their perilous escape as a "grand night," courageously ignoring the dangers of wind and wave.

Alone in a foreign country, pregnant and unmarried, facing an uncertain future in their internment in Switzerland (comfortable though they are), Catherine remains the gentle leader, sensitive to Frederic's isolation, inactivity, and possible boredom. Without being an unbelievable paragon, she is self-deprecating and kind, and above all she is brave, perhaps as women who deliver babies must be brave. But Frederic has recognized that quality in her even before her ordeal. Despite the "trap" of biology, Frederic had said their love would endure outside interference "Because you're too brave." Catherine had contradicted him but added she would like to be brave. Frederic then qualified his judgment and claimed a lesser degree of bravery for himself, but he had insisted on Catherine's bravery. "No," she replies. "But I hope to be" (139–40).

She had been brave in their escape, and as she begins labor he tells her once more she is brave. Her response is that she is not afraid (313). Indeed, she is excited and cheerful and remains so (abetted by the anesthetic laughing gas). Frederic twice admits his fear, even as he admonishes Catherine to be brave (322–24). Then when she has begun to hemorrhage and they both anticipate her death, she twice says she is unafraid of death, and for the last time he speaks to her: "You dear, brave sweet" (330–31).

Lest we think her characterization is of an unreal, ideal person, there is one telling instance that proves otherwise. Yet in its humanizing of her, the detail lends substance and depth to her character. On coming into her room to talk with her for the last time, Frederic cries and Catherine consoles *him*, but when she says she hates dying, he takes her hand. At that point she tells him, "Don't touch me." That command is rich with suggested meaning, even when she immediately counters it with a return to her usual solicitous nature: "Poor darling. You touch me all you want" (330). It is too late for not touching. Frederic had touched her once too often. But her instinctive fear may lay behind that one hard order, just as it once more reveals Catherine as strong but vulnerable, complex, and both practical and idealistic.

5.

Presentation

Voice

To perceive what Hemingway makes of Frederic as his narrator, it is necessary to hear Frederic's voice and not just the words he writes and speaks. (Here too it is useful to see that there is a difference as well as a connection between Frederic the character and Frederic the narrator.) Voice is a loosely defined literary concept but a vital one, for it is the medium, or agency, of meaning apart from words considered semantically. In drama we readily perceive voice at work in the different manners in which any two actors will read the same lines. It is not simply that each speaker has a unique acoustical voice but that each speaker *and* writer may shape through various stylistic devices the way or mood in which words are to be understood. Thus, playwrights will sometimes interject directions to guide actors: Fay [*leaning over seriously*]: We think so, Miller; Stella [*mildly*]: Don't holler at me like that; Willy [*furiously*]: Casino!

Frederic uses very few adverbs like these the playwrights use, and he presents many episodes that are dialogic without them. But he does, lightly, describe in places, as in chapter 11, which is mainly dialogue sandwiched between two narrative paragraphs. To unlock the voices of the priest and Frederic here, one must study (a) their characters as presented to this point and (b) their words here, the way sensitive actors and directors would. Indeed, an excellent way of reading fiction for a more thorough understanding of it than silent reading unveils is through the oral interpretation of it.

Frederic's voice, of course, is not unchanging. In different scenes we "hear" different tones in it. But because his is a retrospective narrative, the underlying and dominant voice is consistent. At some point, possibly about 10 years after Catherine's death but certainly at least 2 years after the novel ends in the spring of 1918, Frederic composes his story. The maximum time frame is determined by our knowing that the novel was written in 1928 and revised and published in 1929. The minimum time frame is determined by Frederic's alluding to Babe Ruth as "a pitcher then playing for Boston" (136). The *then* refers to that "present time," September 1917, when indeed Babe Ruth played for the Boston Red Sox; he would be traded to the New York Yankees in 1920, as Frederic, a retrospective narrator, must know. Thus we know that some time has elapsed between the last events of the story and Frederic's composition of it. He is looking back and retrospectively finding a voice to tell the story.

"Voice" exists midway between character and style, which play off each other to create voice.[15] Having examined Frederic's character earlier, we may now consider certain stylistic features associated with voice. Again using the crucial first chapter as illustration, we find Frederic's characteristic voice at the end of it. After a loving description of the things of his world in rhythmical, vivid sentences and paragraphs, in evocative images of the landscape of both nature and warfare, he ends with a frightful two-sentence paragraph: "At the start of the winter came the permanent rain and with the rain came the cholera. But it was checked and in the end only seven thousand died of it in the army" (4).

In H. W. Fowler's famous handbook, *A Dictionary of Modern English Usage,* a useful chart differentiates among the words *humor, wit, satire, sarcasm, invective, irony, cynicism,* and *the sardonic.* The chart does not directly define the terms, but it indicates four classifications for each, and it is *the sardonic* that best describes Frederic's voice here. The "motive or aim" of it is *self-relief;* its "province" is *adversity;* its "method or means" is *pessimism;* and its "audience" is the *self.* The sardonic voice we first hear in chapter 1 is full of portent for the sad tale that follows. Frederic's story is one of persistent adversity that leads him to a pessimistic view of the world but also—and in this change lies his victory—to the very retelling of it that will bring him relief and also us, vicariously, who triumph in the war of the words *through* words.

First-time readers may not know that the camouflage of life that men use to disguise the instruments of death will enlarge into a dominant theme in the novel. Nor can they more than generally know the significance of rain or that the soldiers looking "as though they were six months gone with child" foreshadow the conclusion of Catherine's death in childbirth. But Frederic, the narrator, knows because all the events of his story have transpired *before* he begins the retelling in order to purge his grief and *come to terms* with it. The phrase is wonderfully meaningful and relevant in its sense of "reaching agreement" as well as coming to *words,* finding that agreement of relief in and through language. (And *come to term* also aptly means "reach the end of pregnancy.") If first-time readers can only generally feel the foreboding tone of the unknown narrative voice, the last paragraph and more specifically the single word *only* work brilliantly to reveal a narrator who at *that* time, 1915, was callous and indifferent to death but at *this* time (of the writing of the story) is sensitive and in need of the relief that the sardonic brings.

This dual effect works intermittently throughout the narrative, as if we are hearing from two persons, the narrator as he was then (1915–18) and the narrator as he is now (1920 or later), after having lived his story. In chapter 2 this dual effect comes through in his description of Gorizia: "The town was very nice and our house was very fine. The river ran behind us and the town had been captured very handsomely but the mountains beyond it could not be taken and I was very glad the Austrians seemed to want to come back to the town some time, if the war should end, because they did not bombard it to destroy it but only a little in a military way" (5). The "very handsomely," the curiously put "very glad," and the crowning "military way" all project a sardonic voice, one mocking the military but also mocking himself, that considerably younger, more naive man who subsequently underwent the hard journey he now retells.

Repeatedly, then, Hemingway had to find words to convey the duality that Frederic is. That is, Frederic must be realistic and "in character" both as the man he was and the man he is to become. Occasionally reminding the reader of the retrospective narration and consistently maintaining his sardonic voice, Frederic (created by and acting through Hemingway's skill) controls and unifies the narration. Contrasted to first-time readers, only he knows the outcome of the story, but he can move us inexorably toward it by the *manner* of telling. We are prepared for it also by foreshadowing, but that too is sardonic, and we "know" aesthetically that the end will be tragic. The province of the sardonic being adversity, its method being pessimism, the final loss is inevitable.

Retrospective narration is suggested in several places and ways. Each of the first three chapters identifies distinct (if vague) times: "In the late summer of that year"—1915 (chapter 1); "The next year"—1916 (chapter 2); "When I came back . . . the spring had come"—1917 (chapter 3). The rest of the narrative, then, covers the crisis year of Frederic's growth into manhood from the spring of 1917 to the spring of 1918. As Thoreau would manipulate the dates of his residency at Walden to convey hope and rebirth in his account of it, so does Hemingway increase the bleakness of his narrator's story by framing it between two springtimes, ironically reversing the conventional pattern of rebirth and hope. Similarly, enforcing the retrospection are Frederic's "I remembered" (11) and "I forget" (291), as well as the many instances in between when in dialogue with Catherine and others and in his recollection of his youth (216) the remote past is evoked at the present, the time of writing a story about a less remote past. Frederic's self-consciousness as a retrospective narrator addressing an audience unfamiliar with this tale is revealed in phrases as *as I said:* "I drove back to Gorizia and our villa and, as I said, went to call on Miss Barkley, who was on duty" (24).

Presentation

Another interesting illustration of the manner of telling the story occurs in a stream-of-consciousness passage in which Frederic thinks first about the war and then about Catherine. For both the war and her he expresses his desires, first rambling on about the war and then fantasizing an amorous night with Catherine and concluding, "That was how it ought to be" (36–38). The passage incorporates the theme of *seeming* and *being* throughout, both with the war and with Catherine. The interesting difference is that none of Frederic's wishes relating to the course of the war is realized, but his daydream about Catherine is later very similarly realized at the end of his hospitalization in Milan, including references in both places to the Via Manzoni, a clicking elevator, and Capri wine—as well as to, of course, their lovemaking (151–53).

This pattern of foreshadowing and echoing is a convention of fiction. Chekhov wrote that if an author mentions a pistol at the beginning of an action, it must be fired before the narrative ends. Significantly different here, however, is that Frederic is both Hemingway's protagonist and his narrator. If Frederic is the man to whom things happen, a relatively passive character, he is empowered in this significant, indeed crucial, respect: he decides how to tell his story, and he weaves it magically together, each piece carefully chosen and wrought to fit the overall pattern.

Two other instances remind us of the retrospective self-consciousness of Frederic's narration. At the racetrack he tells us, "They had no elastic barrier at San Siro *then*" and, as mentioned earlier, when reading about baseball in a 1917 newspaper he reminds us, "Babe Ruth was a pitcher *then*" (129, 136; my emphasis). One effect of our awareness of the distance between the narration and the tragic events of the story is to give greater weight to certain points, ever mindful that in a tautly wrought tale each point counts. We thus come to understand, as Frederic himself understands, retrospectively. Once we have read the novel, we can then feel the full weight and significance of the details in the pattern, such as the one in which Frederic—not some remote authorial voice but the protagonist himself—describes the soldiers as looking "six months gone with child" (4). That is his deliberate and his organic choice of words.

We also suspend our disbelief in his capacity to remember the long stretches of dialogue throughout the novel. This tacit agreement is another convention of fiction, one that is less problematical when the author writes from a third-person point of view (especially when the author assumes omniscience). We are not asked to believe that Frederic has total recall or that he records each scene stenographically or immediately afterward. Nonetheless, the convention creates a tension between the requirements that we (a) read the narration as retrospective and (b) read it as vividly realistic. Consider, for instance, a few details in chapter 4. If the coffee was usually "a pale gray and sweet with condensed milk," Frederic's so describing it would not be unusual. But a following detail seems both vivid and immediate: "There was that beginning of a feeling of dryness in the nose that meant that the day would be hot later on" (16). Such details and the long dialogue place us in the midst of a realistic, ongoing action. But when in this same episode Frederic repeatedly (three times) states that the work of his ambulance section went well without him, he indicates the difference between the ongoing action and his reflections on it, just as in several instances (cited earlier) he reminds us that he is *remembering* from some point later than that of the events of the story.

One other such reminder is crucial to perceiving this tension in narration between Frederic when he was younger, gauche and innocent, and Frederic the retrospective narrator with the wisdom gained from the experiences of his story. This reminder is at first somewhat ambiguous in reference, but it is clearly a signal that Frederic's changing viewpoint is important to the tale. Chapter 3 begins the fatal year of 1917, and in that chapter Frederic contrasts the profane love of his recent leave with what is to emerge as the sacred love the priest believes in. Somewhat callously, Frederic "winefully" (whinefully, too) explains to the priest that "*we* did not do the things *we* wanted to do; *we* never did such things" (13; my emphasis). His use of the first-person plural is a way of both generalizing his individual guilt and distancing the narrator from his earlier self. The following long and crucial paragraph begins with remarkably vivid images of the Abruzzi, and it is important to recognize that these are images of a place that, as far as we know, Frederic has never seen. Yet they are more particular than the immediately following images of the cafés and rooms of profane love that he has seen.

Frederic then shifts his viewpoint again, having used the first-person singular to account for the Abruzzi and to recount his leave. He admits his limitation in telling about his leave and particularly the differences between nights and days: "*I* could not tell it; as *I* cannot tell it *now*. But if *you* have had it *you* know. He [the priest] had not had it but he understood. . . . He had always known what I did not know and what, when I learned it, I was always able to forget. But I did not know that *then*, although I learned it *later*. In the *meantime we* were all at the mess. . . . *We* two stopped talking." And finally at the end of the chapter, "*We* all got up and left the table" (13–14; my emphasis).

The passage is remarkable for the shifts both in point of view and in time and place. Yet they are all psychologically apt. First Frederic identifies himself with all other profane lovers who fail to do the "things we wanted to do." In the very next sentence, however, the *we* refers to the priest and himself, together and apart from the others in the mess. Then he shifts to the *I* who imagines the Abruzzi, then to the *I* who "had gone . . . to the smoke of cafés," and then to the second-person *you* by which Frederic invites the reader's participation in his experiences while also making us conscious of the narrative strategy here. He admits to an inadequacy in describing the essence of his experiences, but just as he had used the first-person plural he later uses the second person to invite a duplicity with the profane reader: "But if you have had it you know."

At this point, the priest is set aside—"He had not had it." But he is quickly reunited with Frederic—"we were still friends"—immediately before the key revelation that if the priest did not have knowledge of the mystery of profane love, he does have some as-yet-unspecified knowledge that contrasts with Frederic's. It is the sacred love that one can "learn" through teaching and preaching (and thus that one is "always able to forget") and also learn through the whole person, not just the head, when one is in love.

Being aware of the nuances of Frederic's voice retrospectively telling his story enlarges the significance of much of what he reports. Indeed, if one were to paraphrase many of Hemingway's stories and chapters, they would seem banal and dull. A good instance of this deepening of the significance of otherwise-mundane material can be seen in chapter 23. In it Frederic first tells of his preparations to return to the battlefront from Milan. He next meets Catherine, and they walk through the city, pausing for him to buy a pistol and ammunition. They then take a carriage to the gaudy hotel room that makes Catherine feel unhappy—"like a whore." Yet she quickly recovers her usual cheerfulness, and they dine in the room and presumably make love before engaging in the rambling conversation that ends the chapter. The lovemaking that is the very reason for their going to the hotel and that could be dramatically rendered is merely hinted at: "After we had eaten we felt fine, and then after, we felt very happy" (153).

But it is how the chapter is narrated, not so much what is told, that advances the mundane action in exciting ways. At the beginning of the chapter, Frederic's references to the times when his train would arrive and depart lead to other temporal references in this episode when the protagonists are hyperconscious of the transciency of life. "We'll ski some time," Frederic says, and Catherine refers to the skiing season in Switzerland. Within the two months she cites, they will in fact be in Switzerland, but they will never ski. "Come in a minute," he says at the armorer's shop (148). Within hours of his departure, Catherine says, "We always will be together," obviously expressing her ideal, to which Frederic responds, "Yes, except that I'm going away at midnight" (150). The sardonic reply is characteristic of Frederic, as he often gives a literal response to Catherine's idealistic statements.

After Catherine's brief malaise at feeling like a whore, "in a little *time* the room felt like our own home." That is Frederic's turn to exaggerate, followed by another of Catherine's wishes that will never be fulfilled: "They'll [the management of the exclusive Hotel Cavour] take us in some *time*" and "We have such a fine *time*" (153–54; my emphasis).

Also in the chapter, Frederic reserves a seat in a railway carriage, he and Catherine wait in the rain for a carriage, he looks out the hotel window at carriages going by, and, listening to the rain, he also hears a motorcar honk. These images lead to his remembering lines from Andrew Marvell's poem "To His Coy Mistress": "But at my back I always hear / Time's wingèd chariot hurrying near." The string of allusions culminates in Frederic's turn to have a touch of malaise. But Catherine points out to him that the poem is not completely apt, for she has not preserved her virginity as the Coy Mistress has. Indeed, she is pregnant, but she cheerfully fends off Frederic's concerned questions and then herself uses sardonic relief by telling him, "We may have several babies before the war is over." To that response, Frederic can only return to the theme of transciency, countering her humorous statement about a seemingly endless war in the macrocosm with his recognition that in their microcosm time marches on: "It's nearly *time* to go." Catherine's response is both syntactically and philosophically unusual but characteristic of her existential courage: "You can *make it time* if you want." The rest of their chapter-ending dialogue is full of references to time, many of them in the future tense, and to the tension between Frederic's acceptance of his duties in the macrocosm and Catherine's willingness to exist apart from that world by making their own time. Frederic simply says, "No," to her Zen-like invitation, and she finally agrees to his insistence that "Time's wingèd chariot" is awaiting him (154–55; my emphasis).

Additional thematic and stylistic details in this typical chapter can be noted. Frederic buys an actual pistol (not Chekhov's exemplary one), and later, when that pistol does go off, it triggers a chain of events in which Frederic does "make it time." His shooting at the disobedient sergeants (chapter 29) is the apex of his absurd loyalty to the macrocosm. In the next chapter (30), his own rebellious soldiers both in talk and by deed prepare Frederic for his own desertion.

Chapter 23 also alludes to the sacred love the priest represents, but only indirectly, through the allusory method of narration. Two buildings contrast, the cathedral at the beginning of the chapter and the hotel at the end. At the cathedral, Catherine and Frederic see a couple like themselves, "a soldier with his girl . . . his cape around her." Frederic mentions the comparison, but Catherine denies it. Yet as they walk through the dark streets she imitates the couple, taking the action the soldier had by embracing Frederic with his cape wrapped around them. Presumably she had denied the comparison because she had also denied the "fine" cathedral as a place for her. She declines Frederic's invitation to enter the cathedral, and when he says the other couple should have some place to go, she says they do: "They have the cathedral," the edifice of sacred love, the priest's place (147).

On the other hand, Catherine and Frederic cross a bridge (metaphoric and real) and choose the bordellolike hotel for making profane love that momentarily distresses her. But after a profane communion meal, they feel good and at one point ask each other absurd questions about real and metaphoric fathers: "[Frederic:] Have you a father?" "[Catherine:] Haven't you a father?" "[Frederic:] No" (154). Biological fathers, stepfathers, priests who are called father (72), the god who is both profanely invoked and prayed to by the dying Passini and by Frederic himself as Catherine dies (55, 330)—all are present throughout the story in ways both subtle and obvious. At the end of this chapter, the Catherine who rejected the cathedral only to find herself cheapened by the hotel into feeling like a whore accepts by an act of courageous will the hotel room as "our fine house," "our home," and transforms their profane love into sacred love simply by declaring, "I'm so very happy married to you"—the expectant father of her baby (154–55).

In a chapter full of reflexive form, and notably Catherine's willed transformation, the reflective mirrors are most apt. At the armorer's shop where Frederic buys a pistol, Catherine asks him, "What are those little mirrors set in wood for?" "They're for attracting birds," he tells her and explains how the Italians thereby lure and shoot larks. "You don't shoot larks do you, darling, in America?" she asks. "Not especially," he laconically answers, and suddenly Catherine feels better (149).

Just as suddenly she feels unhappy confronted by the "many mirrors" in the hotel room. She is the bird (also meaning "young woman") lured and about to be shot: "She saw herself in one of the mirrors and put her hands to her hair. I saw her in three other mirrors. She did not look happy" (152). But by her will and through her love she accepts her circumstances and satisfies her appetite, by dining on woodcock (another "game" bird), and then even the mirrors become "very attractive," as she sardonically notes (153).

In terms of retrospective narration, throughout the chapter we hear Frederic's voice reminding himself of the fog "turning to rain," the "drops of water" on the carriage driver's coat and his hat "shining in the wet," the "long ride . . . in the rain," the "raining . . . and the horse steaming in the rain," and finally, in the hotel room, "we were very still and we could hear the rain" (150–54). This episode occurs midway through the story. Chapter 1 ends with reference to the "permanent rain" of a northern Italian winter (4), and the very last word of the novel is "rain" (332). The naturalistic details of rain impart realism, but beyond that function, having been experienced, remembered, and *told* by Frederic, they assume a function like the drone of a bagpipe, uniting the parts of the story with their underlying associations for him of death, loss, and suffering. Similarly, because *he* heard, remembered, and told Catherine's words, what was then banal and casual now resonates with meaning in retrospect. At the end of their hotel interlude, Catherine wishes to allay Frederic's concerns for her. She will arrange having the baby: "Don't worry, darling. We may have several babies before the war is over" (155). Her brave, sardonic humor in the face of a grim, seemingly endless war is recalled and told by Frederic from the vantage point of a cruel knowledge they did not then have.

Point of View

Another interesting feature of the way in which Hemingway has Frederic recall and narrate the story has already been touched on in chapter 4's section on Frederic's character. As he develops in the course of the story, his point of view shifts, as the changing referents of pronouns indicate. First, for example, he identifies with his profane fellow officers but then also sees himself and the priest as having a special relationship. Later he and Catherine become the dominant *we* of the story. At other places the shifting point of view reveals further growth in Frederic's character, growth reflected by his choice of pronouns.

When he buys a pistol for himself, he says to Catherine, "Now we're fully armed" (149). Including her (rather than excluding her with "Now I'm fully armed," a more logical form) perhaps indicates his sensitivity to Catherine's feeling "terrible" on their last night together before his return to the front. "Now we're fully armed" suggests they will be together in spirit just as it suggests the irony of being armed in a story of farewell to arms. (Later Catherine returns the favor when she tells him, "I suppose if we really have this child we ought to get married," the first *we* including him in an act in which he is superfluous [293]).

Another passage contains several shifts in grammatical person that reflect changes in Frederic's view of the war. Formerly, *we* were the Italians and *they* were the Austrians in clear-cut opposition (for example, in chapter 2), but as the war dragged on and the moral questions were no longer clear-cut, the referents change. The war profiteers, the bungling leaders, the officious, and the selfish are revealed, and they are on "our" side. The enemy is remote and behaves militarily in predictable ways. On the retreat, then, the *we* is reduced to Frederic and his small group of men, and the *they* at times are the Italians as well as the attacking Germans, foreshadowing Frederic's trial by *them:* "they would shoot us for Germans. They shot Aymo." Next Frederic's memory shifts the *we* to some anonymous companions in the remote past, and then to the second person—"You could not go back"—as if inviting the reader to join him in recognizing a universal truth of the futility of restoring the nostalgically recalled past. Subsequently Frederic's small group is further reduced by the desertion of Bonello, and the referents become *I* and *he* (Luigi Piani, his last driver). His alienation is pushed to the breaking point when he loses the comfort of *we* as he is pulled away from Piani by the battle police. It is then Frederic alone versus them: "I saw how their minds worked; if they had minds and if they worked. They were all young men and they were saving their country." Then he shifts back to an identification with another *we*, but it is not with Catherine or even with his drivers that he identifies; it is with his fellow victims: "They wore steel helmets. Only two of us had steel helmets. . . . We stood in the rain and were taken out one at a time to be questioned and shot" (224).

Of course, the next shift is to mark his "separate peace," and thus he will break his identification with the other victims and as "I" run for the river and escape by diving into its swollen waters. But yet another shift occurs in these few pages, and again it is not merely grammatical but functional in a subtle way. Throughout the novel Frederic has demonstrated his eye for nature and particularly trees. In chapter 1 he notes trees and their leaves, "many orchards," and "a forest of chestnut trees," just as he notes (apropos the theme of false-real and disguise) that the cut branches of trees are used to camouflage the destructive artillery. This contrast between the living and the dead is repeated in chapter 2, when he again notes the chestnut forest, "many thick shady trees in a walled garden," and "the long avenue of trees." On the other hand, "The forest of oak trees on the mountain beyond the town was gone. The forest had been green in the summer . . . but now there were the stumps and the broken trunks and the ground torn up" (3–6).

He continues to note trees like the cypresses, trees symbolic of mourning, lining the road to the villa where Catherine lives (41). And rambling on about his wishes once in the wineful mess hall and linked with the priest's invitation to the Abruzzi (a wooded mountain region), he says he also wanted to go to the Black Forest and the Harz Mountains, other wooded regions. Thus, the shift from the "I" who escapes to the "we" of the desperate swim downstream is aptly identified as Frederic and his savior, "a piece of timber," one of "much wood in the stream. . . . *We* passed the brush of an island above the water" (225; my emphasis).

In beginning the next chapter Frederic again uses the second person, this time in the manner of an informal narrator consciously inviting us to listen and understand: "You do not know how long you are in a river when the current moves swiftly." He then returns to using

"I" and "we": "I was afraid of cramps and I hoped we would move toward the shore. We went down the river in a long curve." Having acted courageously, Frederic is reduced even in that action to a passive role in which he is literally dependent on the timber for support and at the mercy of the current, which provided refuge but is a natural force over which he has no control (225–27).

Similarly, Frederic uses the plural *we* to refer to himself and the railroad flatcar onto which he hops and in which he takes refuge during his escape: "We were almost opposite the bridge. . . . We were past" (229).

Having often noted trees, having expressed concern for the blasted oak forest of the war (6) and the cutover hemlock trees of his youth (215), he is then saved by timber in the saving waters. And in the space of a few pages, as he switches back and forth in point of view, he is wrestling himself free from the ego he was. He joins himself with the world through his seeing trees and railroad cars as being linked to him as surely as his friends and Catherine. He thus recognizes the failure or the philosophical insufficiency of egoism. And at the beginning of chapter 32, immediately after his joining himself with a piece of timber and a flatcar, he further sees even his body as not entirely his own. One of his knees, his head, and the inside of his belly are his, but he concedes his other knee to the surgeon, Dr. Valentini, and does not lay claim to anything else. His very body, as his mind, is becoming universalized. Most ironically, as he makes his separate peace, he unites himself to the world (231).

6.

Some Themes

Crazy

One aspect of Catherine's character that broadens out into a motif first forms a connection to Frederic's character and then ties in with a central theme of the novel. When Frederic makes his first pass at Catherine, her reactions, initially slapping him and then yielding to his embrace and kiss, leads Frederic to conclude that she is unbalanced. When she acts as if they are committed lovers, he thinks, "[S]he was probably a little crazy," and Catherine confirms his diagnosis: "You see I'm not mad and I'm not gone off. It's only a little sometimes" (30–31). Throughout the novel both she and Frederic refer to these first encounters as a time when her behavior was "crazy" as she tried to deal with the death of her fiancé and to shape a new life for herself in the dislocations, physical and mental, of war.

In Milan, after Frederic has changed from being her mere seducer to her sincere lover, Catherine recalls, "I haven't been happy for a long time and when I met you perhaps I was nearly crazy. Perhaps I was crazy" (116). Later that summer she confesses to her fear of the rain that Frederic, in contrast, likes. When she says she sometimes sees herself and Frederic dead in the rain, he gently chides her, "I don't want you to get Scotch and crazy tonight," to which she replies, "[B]ut I am Scotch and crazy." And despite her *knowing* that "It's all nonsense," she cannot help *feeling* a powerful premonition of doom brought on by the rain that is, of course, falling again at her death (125–26).

When Frederic is about to return to the front, the topic of one of their last conversations is again this craziness. Although Catherine now alleges she is "a very simple girl," she admits she "was a little crazy. But I wasn't crazy in any complicated manner. I didn't *confuse* you, did I, darling?" (my emphasis). Most interestingly, Frederic chooses to ignore the question and instead talks of the wine they are drinking; then, his head "very clear and cold" he wants "to talk facts." Catherine once more turns the tables on Frederic and gives him only general, vague answers to his two questions searching for "facts" about her pending childbirth. She does answer his third question precisely; she will write "Every day." But she echoes her unanswered question, whether she'd *confused* him, by saying she will write "very confusing" letters to confound the censors reading his mail (154–55). The humorous conversation reveals Catherine's playful good spirits just as it does Frederic's growing sense of responsibility and apprehension. But lexically it broadens the theme of *craziness* to include *confusion*. Now, however, it is the formerly "crazy" Catherine who will use guile to protect their privacy.

Toward the end of the story the topic of Catherine's early imbalance once more comes up. The memory of it is important to her and is in her waking thoughts: "I was nearly crazy when I first met you," she says. To this Frederic replies, "You were just a little crazy." Catherine's response insists on her present happiness and stability: "I'm never that way any more. . . . And I'm not crazy now. I'm just very, very, very happy" (300). As if to prove it, she then suggests they return to sleep at the same time. "But we did not," and Frederic lies awake "thinking about things and watching Catherine sleeping, the moonlight on her face" (301).

Their mental lives have crossed paths. Frederic's love has "cured" Catherine of her craziness brought on by the craziness of the war that killed her fiancé. Catherine's love has "cured" Frederic of his irresponsibility and thoughtlessness. Love has brought Catherine happiness, but it has brought Frederic a new awareness of the crazy context of his life. If the repeated references to Catherine's private craziness seem to focus the theme on her and the curing power of love, Frederic also becomes increasingly aware of the public craziness that at first he was indifferent to or dismissed with irony. Of 1915 he remembered and chooses to note sardonically that "*only* seven thousand died" of cholera (4; my emphasis), and in 1917, discussing the war with Catherine, she politely disagrees with him as they both use the idiomatic "crack" to refer to the point at which either a person or a nation becomes dysfunctional. The war will end because "It will crack somewhere," Frederic says, and Catherine says, "We'll crack. . . . They can't go on doing things like the Somme and not crack" (20). It was at the "ghastly show" (18) of the bloodbath at the Somme river in France in 1916 where her fiancé was slain, and *she* "cracked" as a result of it. When Frederic avers (falsely, as it turns out) that the Italians will not "crack," Catherine disagrees, and her reply is redolent with allusion to her own experience: "They [the Italians] may crack. . . . Anybody may crack" (20).

After the first years of the war, when the participants fought under old illusions about the gallantry of battle, most of them have come to see that instead of being knights in shining armor, perhaps returning to their lovers with "picturesque" wounds, they are powerless victims of a monstrous brutality (20). Catherine's craziness and subsequent understanding are the direct result of it. Frederic's education begins with her story and is continued by his other "tutors"—his ambulance drivers, the priest, Rinaldi, and even strangers, such as a barber and Catherine's doctor. Frederic's driver and articulate advocate of peace, Passini, analyzes the war and its underlying reasons and concludes that he and his antiwar comrades "will convert him"— Frederic (48–51). Within minutes of his tutoring, Passini is dead, his senseless and bloody death like Catherine's fiancé's: "They blew him all to bits" (20, 55). The anonymous "they" aptly suggests the impersonal horror of mechanized, long-range, high-explosive war. But before his death, Passini had told Frederic that fear and going "crazy" are the factors that continue the war (50).

Early on, Frederic jokingly tells his friend Rinaldi that he is crazy (65), but as the war drags on Rinaldi admits to Frederic that "This war is killing me" and repeats that "This war is terrible" (167–68). He is driven to excessive drinking, thinks he has syphilis, and admits to his mess-hall companions, "I'm just a little crazy" (174).

Much that could be characterized as craziness or unreason subsequently takes place, but the word itself is used by Frederic to describe the disastrous retreat in which bridges are not blown and defenses are not set. Expecting reason, Frederic becomes "very angry"—again at an anonymous "they"—and tells his men, who all along have been trying to make him see it, that "The whole bloody thing is crazy" (211).

In a humorous but foreshadowing counterpoint to the battlefield disaster that includes Frederic's shooting an Italian sergeant, other Italians killing Frederic's friend Aymo, and Frederic's nearly being executed, Frederic is also at risk because of a similar confusion. When he is in the Milan hospital, his barber mistakes him for an Austrian officer, and Frederic thinks, "If he was crazy, the sooner I could get out from under the razor the better" (90). In a sense, the barber *is* crazy, confused, mistaken—as many of the characters are in varying ways. Freshly shaved by a crazy barber, Frederic then sees Catherine after their separation, and now he too is crazy, but crazy through not fear or hate but love:

> "I'm crazy about you. . . ."
> "I'm just mad about you. . . ."
> "I'm crazy in love with you."

And Catherine confirms that their making love in his hospital room "was just madness" (92). Perhaps that craziness, that madness, considering its fatal consequences, was not so different from the other sorts.

Finally, the theme is incidentally present in the couple's hotel room in Stresa when Frederic's friend the barman comes to warn him that he is to be arrested in the morning. "Is the barman crazy?" Catherine asks, for throughout the novel people act and think unreasonably, and apart from the motif inherent in repeated words like *crazy* and *madness,* the theme merges with other motifs. Because the war *is* crazy, becoming crazy may be an ironic turn into an almost-unbearable wisdom.

Appearance versus Essence: Guise and Disguise

The theme is present in other ways, and it is clearly a central philosophical question: What is real as opposed to what is illusion? Put simply, what is true and what is false? The questions are not merely academic, because in the drama of the novel they affect lives in profound ways. Indeed, if one ignores and disdains confrontation with these questions, one does not escape the consequences of such indifference or ignorance; one's life is instead inauthentic. In Hemingway's fiction, one may act and strive and cope, but one is not fully human, an authentic being, until one can see beyond appearance to essence, both in one's own character and in the world of other persons, other things. Perhaps this fullness or authenticity is inherent in the capacity to love or otherwise see beyond one's own selfish interests and basic needs to an awareness of and life within a community.

In any case, *A Farewell to Arms* is a story above all about Frederic Henry's growth in such understanding and toward authenticity. And because it is *his* story we must always be mindful that *he* reports those events, describes those characters and places which contribute to the central effect. Thus, for instance, at the end of the story Catherine's doctor misspeaks when he tells her, "You are not going to die." He compounds his error when he, the silly one, tells her, "You must not be silly," and for all his good intentions he wants to change the essence of the experience by telling Frederic "The operation proved—"and Frederic cuts him off and attempts without success to say good-bye to Catherine's body (331–32). Frederic refuses to sentimentalize, to falsify, or to digress to a discussion of the operation that would possibly relieve the doctor but divert tragedy to technocracy.

At the other end of the story we are immediately given the theme in the brilliant first chapter, but it is disguised in the description that functions on the level of *setting,* as the narrator places us and launches us into the story. The vivid description of the first paragraphs of the novel contain two telling details of disguise or illusion. The camouflaged artillery—the weapons of death "covered with green branches . . . and vines"—and the soldiers whose ammunition gives the narrator the illusion that "they were six months gone with child" foreshadow the tragic end when, in the act of hoping to give life, Catherine dies, the lethality of the soldiers' cartridges becoming analogous to the stillborn baby.

In between the seemingly innocent but foreboding beginning and the tragic ending, Frederic repeatedly tells us of a world turned upside down. The military use of camouflage is referred to several times, as is the growth or dormancy of vegetation. Frederic is attracted to such details, just as he is to the turning of the seasons and daily weather (for example, 3, 128, 185). The natural world attracts him, but he also notices how it is used by war to disguise or falsify for destructive or protective purposes. The exposed road where he must drive his ambulances is screened from enemy observation by cornstalks and straw matting that incongruously make it seem to Frederic "like the entrance at a circus or a native village." Similarly, the dressing station for wounded soldiers is in the ovens of a brickyard (46), and its entrance is sheltered by some green branches that Frederic notes both before and after his wounding (51, 57). The green, leafy bower that in pastoral literature is a place of repose and love is here transformed into a place of carnage where doctors soaked in blood try to salvage mangled bodies. At the time of his second disaster of war, the Caporetto retreat, Frederic again notes the use of vegetation to conceal the Italians' road movements (181, 185). The time of the third and last disaster, Catherine's "false" childbirth, is ushered in by what Frederic notes as a "false spring" (310). The natural world itself seems deceptive or is perceived by Frederic as illusory.

Also contributing to the overall ambiguity of the real and the false is the motif of theatricality. On the one hand is "real" life; on the other, the "false" life of theater and opera and, by extension of the analogy, even war. Battles are thought of as "shows." The understatement reduces the real fear and danger in the minds of those at risk to an entertainment at which one is a passive spectator. Frederic first uses this word to name the Somme battle in which Catherine's fiancé was blown to bits: "It was a ghastly show" (18). When Frederic later visits Catherine en route to the front, he says, "I'm leaving now for a show up above Plava," and Catherine's response is questioning and skeptical: "A show?" (43). When Frederic finally deserts, he thinks of the entire war as "not my show any more" (232). After their escape from Italy, Catherine and Frederic act out roles in order to be given asylum in Switzerland, and the scene with the Swiss officials concludes successfully with Frederic telling Catherine, "It's like a comic opera today" (285).

Before the Italian front collapses, Frederic thinks of it as "picturesque" (20) and his role in the war as being somewhat theatrical. When he returns from leave, he discovers that he really is supernumerary (a term with both military and theatrical associations). Although he thought he was essential, his unit had functioned well without him, had indeed even "seemed to run better while I was away" (16). When he is involved in the planning for an attack, his role is unessential but gives him "a false feeling of soldiering" (16–17), and he concedes to Catherine that he is not really in the army: "It's only the ambulance" (18). Frederic thinks that the Italian form of saluting is theatrical and their uniforms beautiful (18, 23), and the rules about wearing helmets and carrying pistols make one seem "too bloody theatrical" (28). In fact, Rinaldi carries toilet paper in his pistol holster (reminiscent of G. B. Shaw's chocolate soldier), and Frederic's real pistol, with its "ridiculous" barrel and ballistics, makes him feel "a vague sort of shame" (29). At this stage, the entire war seems like "war in the movies"—undangerous, unreal. And even after his wounding and during the retreat from Caporetto, Frederic sees the sergeants as "unshaven but still military *looking*" (199; my emphasis). That is, as the sergeants shortly demonstrate by running away, there is a profound difference between seeming and being.

Supporting and enlarging this motif is the seemingly tangential subplot focusing on the American opera singer Ralph Simmons. He really is a character in theater, whereas Frederic is playing roles on a stage of real blood and death. But Simmons still reflects the seeming-being duality because there is some question as to his ability, and apart from his "roaring" into an aria from Giacomo Meyerbeer's once-popular *L'Africana,* no one of the characters actually hears him sing (242). Further, he has a disguise—that of his stage name, which curiously echoes Frederic's last name, Enrico DelCredo, literally (in English) Henry of the Creed (or belief or faith) (119–21). Presumably, he and the other American singer, Saunders, have adopted Italian stage names because of stereotypes—forms of seeming-being in which one does not expect Americans but does expect Italians to be good opera singers.

In this episode another minor character helps develop the related motif of national identity, one more way by which one is known. Is Ettore Moretti an Italian or an American? Clearly Frederic is an American in the Italian army. Ettore is his foil in many ways. Although he too is an American in the Italian army, Ettore has cultural duality as an Italian American. He speaks idiomatic American English and claims fluency in Italian, mocking Simmons and Saunders for their poor Italian and pointing out to Frederic that his limited Italian will keep him from the promotion Ettore will receive. Most significantly different, however, are Ettore's attitudes. He is the miles gloriosus of the story, conceited, bragging, and boring, and Catherine contrasts him with Frederic, whom she likes exactly as he is (124–25).

Another character with dual nationality is the ruptured soldier whom Frederic tries to help. This Italian American, unlike Ettore, wants to avoid hazardous duty, but Frederic's attempt to help him is frustrated. Just as questionable national identities may lead to peril or confusion, so does the self-inflicted (false) wound lead to failure (33–36). Nothing seems to serve the purpose or reason of Frederic.

Catherine and her friend Helen Ferguson further illustrate the ambiguity of identity through nationality because they are Scottish, a nationality without a nation, now a part of the United Kingdom of Great Britain but retaining their own sense of a separate cultural identity. The Italians in the novel fail to understand the distinction, however, since all the nurses speak English. And when Frederic is inquiring of Catherine's whereabouts, he asks not for the Scottish but for the

English lady (240). The distinction leads Rinaldi to some humorous confusion when he is talking to Helen Ferguson, who insists on her separate cultural identity as Scottish (20–21).

Frederic feigns surprise at the English ambulance driver's self-identification as English: "Did you think I was Italian?" he asks Frederic (58).

But it is Frederic himself who best illustrates the motif. At various points in the novel he is taken to be Italian, French, Austrian, German, or South American. Rinaldi knows Frederic is American but thinks of him as being essentially Italian in character (66). When Catherine initially meets Frederic, her first question after her greeting is "You're not an Italian, are you?" (18). Perhaps his salute, more moderate than Rinaldi's, prompts her question. At his wounding, one of the doctors is surprised to learn Frederic is American: "I always thought he was French" (60). The barber in the hospital thinks he is Austrian (90–91), and the Italian rear guard fire on Frederic and his men, killing Aymo, assuming they are German infiltrators (214). Similarly, Frederic reasons that the Italian battle police will assume his accented Italian will reveal him as a German in disguise (222–24). These seeming-being confusions are fatal or near-fatal and are foreshadowed by the earlier mistaken beliefs, such as those of the sergeants who believe that Frederic, like Ettore and the ruptured soldier, must be an Italian from North or South America. When they are told the truth, they "did not believe it" (195). At one point even Catherine teases Frederic about being an Othello, a foreign (Moorish) soldier protecting the Republic of Venice. Although she cannot know it and Frederic resists the comparison, Catherine, like Othello's Desdemona, will also die for love after her soldier-lover abandons his arms for hers (257).

Count Greffi knows Frederic is American, and he, like Othello, served both his own country and another, Austria (254). In their conversation the Count, whom Frederic thinks of as wise (and at 94, he is certainly of wide experience), suggests that an underlying reason for Frederic's malaise is his isolation from his fellow Americans: "One misses one's countrymen and especially one's countrywomen. I know that experience" (260). He also judges that the war among the nations is "stupid," a thematic variant of *crazy* (262), and that thought of his relates to and reinforces the central and essentially pacifistic theme of the novel. National identities and loyalties are one thing, but when they lead to chauvinism and a false patriotism they are murderous, crazy, stupid. What does one's homeland mean or represent? The wise Count suggests that one should love one's fellow citizens and that abstract values can delude one into false patriotism, acting foolishly in behalf of illusions.

Frederic, of course, is not a man without a country, but he is uprooted, alienated from it and from his people, whom we know so little about because he thinks of them so little. The nameless priest, Rinaldi, a few of his men, Count Greffi, and the barman seem to constitute a small alternate community that shrinks even further when in his love for Catherine and in the threat to his life Frederic flees Italy to live in virtual isolation with her. Their existence is most unusual (if not "false"), yet it well illustrates the romantic dream of finding happiness in the profound love of only one individual. An alternative path to happiness is nonetheless implicit in his story.

In his reverie during a pause in the retreat, Frederic momentarily draws aside the curtain hiding a past communal life. The reverie strangely emerges from his thoughts of his current crisis and the death of his friend Aymo, the driver he was closest to. The thoughts of a remote time and place are triggered by the psychological association of the barn and hay in Italy with a barn and hay of his youth. This nostalgia is for a past that is gone and irretrievable, but it is an important revelation nevertheless of his desire (216). Further, this elegiac longing is also illustrated in the priest's descriptions of his beloved home in the mountainous Abruzzi region of Italy, an area isolated in both time and place, a pastoral haven remote from both the war and the cities of the plains that attract the profane. We first hear of it when Frederic is about to go on leave and his fellow officers are suggesting where he should go, as "to centres of culture and civilization" or places where he can "have fine girls" (8). Instead, the priest urges Frederic to go to his Abruzzi, where the hunting and the people are good and the weather is cold, clear, and dry (9).

Some Themes

Frederic's rejection of the invitation hurts the priest. Both the priest, who knows the Abruzzi intimately, and Frederic, who knows it only by the priest's descriptions, have idealized it. Yet even if it is seen through rose-colored glasses, the Abruzzi has a significant place within the overall pattern of the false versus the real love of one's own country and one's own countrymen and women. After the two early descriptions of the Abruzzi (chapters 2–3), it is etched in Frederic's remorseful memory as the land of heart's desire. It is the very place that represents the ambiguous difference between the priest-as-tutor and Frederic-as-student.

The passage at the end of chapter 3 is thematically of the greatest importance even with its tantalizing ambiguity. Here Frederic, although he does not explain what the priest knew or what those *its* refer to, is clearly to pass from ignorance to awareness because of the symbolic function of the Abruzzi, the homeland where nature and human beings cohere, where life is good.

After Frederic's wounding, both Rinaldi and the priest visit him in the field hospital. Both are his friends, both bring gifts, and both have conversations with him that in part are meant to be instructive. But Rinaldi is the profane tutor; the priest, the sacred one. Rinaldi is at first bubbling over with news of Frederic's expected decorations for his part in the successful attack, his own successes as a surgeon, and the good quality of the cognac he has brought. But when Frederic asks him about Catherine and the women in the brothel, Rinaldi's joy changes to comic criticism of both the sex objects who have become friends and the anonymous exploiters who administer the brothel. His talk continues in a mocking, ribald vein, first suggesting that Frederic and the priest are lovers and then criticizing Frederic for his attraction to Catherine, "Your lovely cool goddess" (66). He then undertakes to advise Frederic on his behavior with Catherine, and Frederic answers him with irritation disguised in irony that does not escape Rinaldi: "Don't be angry, baby" (67). In friendly debate, they each accuse the other of ignorance, but Rinaldi repeatedly asserts their brotherhood and even says Frederic is not American but essentially Italian (66). Rinaldi's wisdom is secular, profane, and the result of hedonistic attitudes about which Frederic seems skeptical, even if he does not challenge them.

On Rinaldi's departure, the next episode concerns the priest's visit, and it contrasts wonderfully. Whereas Rinaldi was all bustle, joy, and vehemence, the priest is embarrassed, tired, and restrained. Although both Rinaldi and the priest are Frederic's good friends, the priest insists on Frederic's differentness and not his brotherhood. Whereas the priest is depressed and hates the war, Frederic does "not mind it"—does "not see it" (70). This somewhat ambiguous *it* refers to the madness and craziness of the war, and clearly Frederic at this point has not questioned his role in it. Indeed, the priest calls him a *patriot* at the same time that he calls him a *foreigner* (71). It is a most ironic juxtaposition that points out the absurdity of nationalism or patriotism based on unquestioned abstractions. Frederic has given no evidence of his love for Italy or for people or things Italian. Indeed, quite the opposite is illustrated in his avoidance of the theatricality of the Italian military. He does have an appreciation of Italian nature, but it is not apart from his appreciation of nature in general, as demonstrated by his later life in Switzerland. And, of course, nature can be characterized only by human beings, as with the "American elm" or "Russian olive." Biology salutes no flag. And although Frederic and Rinaldi are friends, clearly they are unlike in many ways. Rinaldi too will eventually yield to the angst of the war and try to immunize himself from it by steeping himself in his bloody profession and the anodynes of sex and alcohol. But he will not learn as Frederic does.

During the priest's visit Frederic once more thinks of an ideal place. If he cannot (for whatever unexpressed reason) return to his childhood haven, he can still imagine with the priest a timeless place where nature and people exist in harmony and where there is none of the madness of their present life. Merely thinking about the possibility of returning to the Abruzzi transforms the depressed priest, who is "suddenly very happy" (71). The priest associates the Abruzzi with human community and the love of God, and he admonishes Frederic to love God and to love others. Frederic denies his capacity to love in the selfless, serving way in which the priest believes, and he also rejects the priest's suggestion that he is unhappy.

As at the end of chapter 3, an ambiguous *it* suggests the transcendent love the priest wishes Frederic to have: "It is another thing. You cannot know about it unless you have it," says the priest. "Well. . . . If I ever get it I will tell you," Frederic replies somewhat facetiously (72). But when the priest suggests that he should leave, Frederic urges him to stay and asks if loving a woman would correspond to the feelings the priest has for and associates with the Abruzzi. Clearly Frederic is curious about the priest's feelings, but he is skeptical and patronizing too, calling him "a fine boy" (72). If the priest is his tutor, Frederic is not yet ready to learn from him. The priest in turn pats Frederic's hand in his farewell, his own patronizing gesture as these two friends' sacred and profane beliefs are juxtaposed in friendly strife.

But the chapter ends not with Frederic summarily noting—as at the end of the prior chapter about Rinaldi's visit—"He was gone" (67) but with Frederic thinking about the priest, whom he liked "very much," and about his beloved Abruzzi, here present in many images in Frederic's mind. The details cohere in the images of "trout in the stream below the town," the serenading of the young men to susceptible young women, the politeness and hospitality of the peasants, and the honor, morality, and loveliness of the isolated region where the birds and the people are all good (73). It is a remarkable reverie of an Edenic place that despite Frederic's denials to the priest indicates the priest has succeeded in implanting his ideals in his student's mind. If nationalism is absurd and destructive, love of place is not. Nationalism leads to disunity, wherein various nations place their interests before collective or international goals. Love of place, on the other hand, may invite the people of it into a community, sharing the resources of the land with grace and dignity. Such love cannot be of a large nation-state, complex and various and tending in its representations to abstractions, generalities, and stereotypes. Within a bioregion, however, one is not lost in "the lonely crowd" but shares in a new tribalism with one's fellow creatures, human and nonhuman.

The confusion about Frederic's actual nationality (French? English? South American Italian?) helps make the point about his being metaphorically a man without a country. He will eventually desert the army that is the main power of the Italian nation, just as many Italians actually did and just as some of his own men urge him to do. Indeed, his men constitute another group of tutors in their reversal of his leadership role. The night of his wounding they try to "convert" him from nationalism:

> "Why don't we stop fighting? . . . They [the enemy] have their own country. . . ."
> "There is a class that controls a country that is stupid and does not realize anything and never can. . . ."
> "Also they make money out of it. . . ."
> "They are too stupid." (50–51)

The persuasion is apparently not lost on Frederic, for he tolerates their seditious talk, ironically calls them "patriots" (53), and then witnesses the frightful death of one of them, the gentle Passini, as if in cruel demonstration of the men's conclusions.

Later another group of his Italian drivers will similarly "teach" Frederic about the madness of nationalism and its wars. On the retreat, they joke about killing an authority figure (the sergeant) who nevertheless was (as Frederic will be soon) a deserter. The men have a certain excitement about their prospect of returning to their hometown, Imola, which figures for them as the Abruzzi does for the priest:

> "By Christ it's a fine place, Tenente. You come there after the war and we'll show you something. . . ."
> "Is it a fine town?"
> "Wonderful. You never saw a town like that. [In it] Everybody is a socialist."

Regardless of the room one might leave for exaggeration in such talk, the point of it reveals the deracinated protagonist among men who have a love for a home and for its people, who share their values. Surely the concluding invitation in the episode—"You come, Tenente.

We'll make you a socialist too"—registers on Frederic's imagination like the priest's invitation, also never realized, to visit the Abruzzi (208).

If Imola and the Abruzzi are not visited, Frederic and Catherine do finally reach a haven in Switzerland, and their winter together on a Swiss mountainside is a realization of Frederic's vision of the Abruzzi (73). If the details are changed—there being no trout stream, no bears, no young men serenading—the quality of the couple's life seems very good in the hands of their hosts, the Guttingens. The descriptions of the place and Frederic and Catherine's life together are equally idyllic: "It was a fine country" and "We had a fine life" (303, 306). Like the Abruzzi, the place where they live is mountainous, wooded, cold, clear, and clean in the winter; is inhabited by happy, friendly people; and is a place of plenty but without extremes of wealth and poverty.

The only unhappiness Frederic feels in their mountain haven is occasioned by his knowledge that the war grinds on: "The papers were bad reading. Everything was going very badly everywhere" (292). And although he doesn't "want to think about the war," he does, and he particularly thinks about the friends he has left behind (298). The timing of Catherine's and the baby's death coincides with various military disasters for the Allies. Just as Frederic and Catherine have left their mountain haven for the city and its hospital, the Germans, already victorious in Italy, begin an offensive in France that Frederic reads about (308). Moreover, at the very hour Catherine begins to hemorrhage, Frederic reads "about the break through on the British front," one more terrible confusion of life and death, one more connection between the war and their lives, as the baby too has broken through the British front (329).

Games: "But Still a Hitter"

Just as camouflage, deceit, and confusion convey the theme of conflict between the false and the real, so does the motif of games do the same. Apart from the common playing of games for recreation and diversion, games seem to have a serious universal function in defining and identifying human beings. Children play at being adults before becoming adults just as staff officers play war games before going to war. The Olympic Games have become a sporting battlefield among nations; defeat for some seems as unacceptable as defeat in war. Again, a confusion exists in using games as a means of transition, preparation, or substitution for something else. On the other hand, games may have an intrinsic value, being worthy for what they are and not as means for something else. Both of these uses of the motif of games are present in the novel.

Early on Frederic perceives the similarity between the war and games or sports. There are two "sides" and a certain randomness to their being chosen. One doesn't belong to or root for a team or a nation so much from rational choice as through chance. Frederic's men perceive the irrationality of the war, the stupidity of their leaders, and the better wisdom of peace because the game of war, unlike true games or sports, may have fatal consequences.

Even after the game proves deadly and Frederic quits the team, he thinks of it in terms of sport: "The war seemed as far away as the football games of some one else's college" (291). But finally he articulates the madness of not just the war but all of life. If the war is confused and crazy, so is all of life, for the result of his and Catherine's love for each other is death, as meaningless and stupid as Aymo's death: "They threw you in and told you the rules and the first time they caught you off base they killed you. Or they killed you gratuitously like Aymo" (327). In the ensuing paragraph Frederic shifts from this analogy to a parable about ants on a burning log, a parable in which the "they" becomes a messiah or potential savior who (like the king, the generals, the battle police, the doctor and nurses, and Frederic himself) proves to be ineffectual. In this game of life, even the winner would take nothing, as Hemingway would suggest in the title of his next volume of short stories, *Winner Take Nothing* (1933).

Throughout the novel sports and games provide ready parallels to other aspects of life. Both are absurd, and if the result is not death, their absurdity or arbitrariness may be recreational. One concedes that a "sporting" way to hunt game birds is to shoot them when they are aloft; the point is not merely to kill the bird but to kill it within certain limits.

Frederic's men Bonello and Piani borrow the language of sport to describe how Bonello killed the sergeant whom Frederic wounded. Indeed, even Frederic's own description of the shooting uses the same wording he might have used in hunting pheasants or quail: "I shot three times and dropped one" (204). By thinking "and dropped one" rather than "and one fell," Frederic (with some readers?) avoids giving agency to the sergeant but keeps himself in the position of subject of the verb. The sergeant, like an incognizant bird, is the mere receiver of Frederic's action. This distancing attitude is confirmed when Bonello brags, "I never killed anybody in this war, and all my life I've wanted to kill a sergeant." But Piani deflates Bonello's cruel boast by using the analogy of unsportsmanlike hunting of birds: "You killed him on the sit all right. . . . He wasn't flying very fast when you killed him" (207).

This episode reveals Frederic as still a willing player of the game of war, even to the point of attempting to summarily kill two sergeants who decide to drop out of the game. Their characterization is slight but revealing: they are conscious of authority and polite (195); they are "unshaven but still military looking" and "good to push" the ambulances should they get stuck (199); one of them is a looter and afraid of being left behind (200); both of them may have selfishly eaten before the others (201); and both are perceived by Frederic as hating him and his men for no specified reason (201). Having been told Frederic is not an Italian officer, the two sergeants seem to lose their ordinary fear of authority, and one of them questions him familiarly and gives him unasked-for advice about resuming the retreat. When one of the ambulances gets stuck in the mud, the sergeants, again selfishly, decide to continue their escape on foot and not help the others dig it out. The one sergeant who tells Frederic that he and his companion "have to go" also tells him, "You can't order us. You're not our officer," while the other remains silent (204). And it is the defiant sergeant whom Frederic aims for and presumably "drops" when they run off. As if in confirmation of this sergeant's base character, we learn that his underwear is dirty when Frederic orders Bonello to strip him of his cape and coat to use as material for traction for the stuck ambulance (205–6).

This episode immediately precedes the chapter in which Bonello, the driver who gives the coup de grace to the sergeant, also deserts, and Frederic, who had shot to kill both sergeants, in his turn deserts. First, under stress and in fear the sergeants had run off. Second, after Aymo dies, Bonello deserts in fear, but Piani and Frederic agree Bonello acted foolishly (218). Third, Frederic's arrest and imminent execution follow, and this succession of events carries a heavily ironic freight. The "sport" of killing a sergeant is immediately followed by gentle Aymo's senseless death, Bonello's senseless desertion, and Frederic's senseless arrest. Each event occurs spontaneously and without premeditation as to consequences. One can distance oneself from reality by participating in games or sport. Seen positively, such activity is re-creation, pleasurable. By definition, there is order to sport and games, that established by rules. True, some people cheat at cards or shoot sitting ducks. But when one plays the game well, within the rules, one has a satisfaction often denied in "real" life when—as here—playing the game, being the good soldier, brings death to Aymo and nearly death to Frederic. One can also distance oneself from the absurdity of reality by using the *language* of games or sport metaphorically, converting the sergeant, no matter how selfish his aims or dirty his underwear, from a man to a game bird. The change makes it *seem* less awful to authorize through the rules of war that one's own teammates (Frederic and Bonello for the sergeant, the battle police for Frederic and other officers) be permitted to "penalize" for infractions of the rules, even to the extreme of death.

Earlier on Frederic had been willing to play outside the rules and to help the ruptured soldier trying to avoid battle (chapter 7). But his Good Samaritan plan had been frustrated. In the retreat, even after Aymo's death, however, Frederic is uncertain as to what he will do about Bonello's desertion, twice telling Piani he doesn't know whether or not he will "umpire" that action, penalize Bonello and his family for that infraction according to the rules. Although Piani pleads with him on pragmatic grounds, it is not until after the retreating soldiers pose a threat to Frederic—an officer who has got them into this mess—that he assures Piani he won't report Bonello's desertion. He will not stick to the absurd rules of war, and his thoughts—like those of the soldiers who hope that the war is over and they are going home—turn to his concern for Piani and his own "home" with Catherine (220–21).

Other instances of the theme of the real versus the false as illustrated in the contrast of arbitrary rules in sports and absurd rules in life (apart from sports and games) are present throughout the novel. The fixed horse racing (chapter 20) is especially important in developing the motif, for it reveals that the corruption of nonsporting life has spread to sports as well. Frederic seems less bothered by the corruption than Catherine, who experiences an existential nausea alleviated only when they act *as if* the corruption does not exist.

At other times when he has leisure, Frederic goes rowing and fishing with the barman in Stresa, and although they catch no fish, Frederic is knowledgeable and instructs the barman in a fishing technique (254–56). Also at Stresa he plays and loses at billiards with 94-year-old Count Greffi, who admits he detects "signs of age now" (259). But even with a handicap, the Count readily beats Frederic. Interestingly, this sporting event stands in contrast to the fixed races in that Frederic and the Count exemplify the honor and ritual of true sport that concludes in friendship and mutual respect (260–63).

When Frederic and Catherine escape to Switzerland, the false-real theme is again present and again occurs through sport. In yet another deceit, the former soldier-architect identifies himself to the Swiss authorities as a sportsman. "Rowing is my great sport. I always row when I get a chance," he says with a straight face, and he and Catherine "want to do the winter sport" (279–80). Their subterfuge is a wonderfully comic occasion for the development of the sport motif, as they then draw the two Swiss officials into a polite debate about the merit of Montreux (one official's hometown) as a good place for winter sport. The first official tells the second that he is "false," and the second tells the first that "accuracy means something," while Frederic, the straight man, *plays* one against the other. It is a harmless, humorous instance of the false-real theme and includes a dispute about the difference between the luge and the toboggan (282–83).

An ironic extension of Frederic and Catherine's deceit is that they both seem truly to like "the winter sport," Catherine wishing she could ski and Frederic wanting to learn to ski. Catherine encourages him to go skiing, and Frederic proposes they go bobsledding (296–97). He does box for exercise, and in doing so he extends the false-real theme by citing the "false" variety of shadowboxing, occasionally frightening the boxing instructor and thinking it "funny" that he should be boxing with a beard (310–11).

Often through the novel Frederic reads newspapers—a narrative device that realistically enables the first-person narrator to know about remote events, such as the course of the war in various "theaters." He almost compulsively reads newspapers, values the ones the priest brings him, reads them regularly when he is alone in the hospital or in bars or restaurants, and even when Catherine is dying reads the newspaper of his neighbor in a café (328–29; see other references to news, newspapers, and magazines on 69, 90, 238, 243, 250, 253, 290–92, 308, 311, 320).

At several points Frederic is ambivalent about the value of newspapers. Early in the novel, this theme is nicely illustrated and tied in with the sport-games motif when, after reading a leading Italian newspaper, the Milan *Corriere della sera,* at dinner, he returns to the hospital to read Boston newspapers left by the American Mrs. Meyers. Although he mentions seeing local news and outdated war news in the papers, he cites only details of sports news and recalls horse-racing events. The key statement in this episode is, of course, not literally true, for he has admitted reading or at least noting a range of topics, yet he tells us, "The baseball news was all I could read and I did not have the slightest interest in it" (135–36). The admission is remarkable, for as he here writes, he is interested enough to include a number of details about baseball, including citations of the Chicago White Sox, the New York Giants, and Babe Ruth. In the 1917 World Series, the White Sox beat the Giants 4–2. The telling point is that at the time of Frederic's retrospectively writing his story, the 1917 White Sox had become the Black Sox of 1919, the team of infamy that had presumably thrown the World Series. Like the fixed horse races of Frederic's 1917 Milan, nothing serves. Even the haven of sports is corrupt. The great American pastime of baseball, a sport made greatly absurd by complicated rules, meaningful beyond ordinary meaning to many Americans because of its rituals and gods, is totally abstracted from one's actual life, totally remote from the political and religious beliefs that usually motivate one. "The baseball news was all I could read and I did not have the slightest interest in it" reveals a man of profound existential dread.

Catherine, however, instinctively perceives the existential courage that enables Frederic to continue to "play the game." Immediately after Frederic's bleak review of the newspapers, Catherine joins him and reveals her pregnancy. That news Frederic "reads" with the greatest interest, and it leads to their strained conversation about the consequences of the pregnancy. Whereas Catherine sees it as "a natural thing," Frederic sees it as part of an inevitable biological trap, a perception that distresses Catherine (138–39). They quickly make up, however, and Frederic repeatedly tells Catherine that she is brave, courageously accepting her condition, pregnant and unmarried in a foreign country at war, her lover about to return to the front where he has already once been nearly killed.

Then Frederic compares himself with a "ball-player that bats two hundred and thirty and knows he's no better." To Catherine, ignorant of baseball, a .230 average seems "awfully impressive," but Frederic disabuses her: "It means a mediocre hitter in baseball." Catherine's answer is powerful: "But still a hitter" (140). She insists on his courage, his willingness to play the game as well as he can, even if he is not equipped to be a hero. As she prepares to leave on her nursing rounds, their exchange neatly returns Frederic to the world and to being a player in it, no matter how absurd or how much a trap: "Perhaps you'll read the papers until I come back," she says, and the episode ends with his compliance. When she returns, he says, "I'll have finished the papers" (141).

The Game of Love

In this novel the most telling extension of the analogy between "real" life and sport and games is in the love of Catherine and Frederic. Love too has its modes and manners, but only when it moves from the private to the public sphere does it move from the realm of custom and individual choice to that of actual law (corresponding to the rules of sport and game). When love is governed by rules, then it too becomes absurd, arbitrary, or irrational. Marriage laws from one country to another vary greatly, even though one might expect similar worldwide religions to provide some commonality. (The divorce laws that govern the end of love are similarly disparate.)

In important ways, *A Farewell to Arms* demonstrates rather than defines what love is, for love—like every other aspect of life and despite the laws of government and the rules of games—is evanescent and ever changing. Ritual, rite, and rule may provide the illusion of solace in religion, a sense of order in government, or even an expectation of safety when one is driving on the right-hand side of the road—though not in Britain. *Around* love, then, we may expect to find as many rules and customs as around baseball or chess, but knowing those rules and customs will never tell what love is, and thus the ambiguity of those passages in which Frederic discusses love with the priest and Count Greffi (13–14, 71–73, 162–63). When Frederic spends his leave whoring or when he and Rinaldi visit the officers' bordello (since a rule says there will be separate bordellos for officers and enlisted men), they are playing at being in love. When the girls in the bordello become friends, Rinaldi regards their relationship as "disgraceful" because it does not imitate the "love" he seeks (65). When Frederic meets Catherine, he immediately sees her as an improvement over the girls in the Villa Rossa, who might satisfy his lust but not gratify his need for sport and game. As Rinaldi perceived, after their visits to the bordello Frederic would have a headache and a bad taste in his mouth from the wine and a bad feeling too in his Anglo-Saxon conscience (168). Fortuitously, Catherine appears on the scene, "quite tall . . . blonde and [with] a tawny skin and gray eyes. I thought she was very beautiful" (18). She lives and works nearby in a "very large and beautiful" villa-hospital. The stage is set for a romantic game, and after he makes a pass at her and she slaps him, he sees his strategy working "like the moves in a chess game" (26). On their next meeting he readily lies to her, telling her he loves her, and sees their relationship as "a game, like bridge, in which you said things instead of playing cards. Like bridge you had to pretend you were playing for money or playing for some stakes. Nobody had mentioned what the stakes were. It was all right with me," at least in part because it is "better than going every evening to the house for officers where the girls climbed all over you and put your cap on backward as a sign of affection between their trips upstairs with brother officers" (30–31). Catherine too seems to have her own motivations for playing the game of love, in her turn using Frederic to assuage the guilt and remorse she feels for the death of her fiancé, making Frederic into a substitute for him. But her weakness is short-lived, and as if she had read Frederic's thoughts about the game of love, she calls time-out: "This is a rotten game we play, isn't it?" she asks. "What game?" he answers, pretending not to understand.

From being a compliant, easy *conquest* (the term suits love, sports, or war) Catherine becomes the reporter of the game and sharply admonishes Frederic: "Don't be dull." Then she patronizes him: "You're a nice boy. . . . And you play it as well as you know how. But it's a rotten game," she insists, and thus she turns the tables on Frederic's planned seduction (31). They will continue to "play," but not the "rotten game" of seduction in which the woman is the "game" pursued by a hunter whose object is to bring her down, to use her for his selfish pleasure. Although at this point Frederic cannot be in love with her, their mutual attraction is the beginning of a relationship that will end in a love of equals when the boy, with his immature, sexist desire, becomes a man.

The game motif is again present at the end of the novel, in book 5, when Catherine and Frederic, he now the hunted in the deadly game of war, come to ground on a mountainside refuge in Switzerland. Not only do their thoughts turn to the sports of bobsledding and skiing, which for them would be noncompetitive and recreational, but one of their first acts is to buy "books and magazines . . . and a copy of 'Hoyle' and [we] learned many two-handed card games" (290). Now their love is played "according to Hoyle"—literally meaning according to the reference book of rules compiled by Edmund Hoyle and still a standard guide and figuratively meaning playing at whatever activity in a fair, honorable way.

The transition between literal games and love is clearly made by both Catherine and Frederic. In one scene he invites her to play chess, and she replies, "I'd rather play with you." For some reason Frederic says, "No. Let's play chess," but when Catherine insists, "And afterward we'll play?" he agrees (300). Hemingway had read T. S. Eliot's major and influential poem *The Waste Land* (1922), and in his novel *The Sun Also Rises,* which preceded *A Farewell to Arms,* thematic parallels to it abound. The second section of the long poem is entitled "A Game of Chess," alluding to two Renaissance plays in which chess is connected to expedient marriage and seduction. Further, Eliot's "A Game of Chess" is partly about a woman who nearly dies in childbirth and is sick from childbearing because her "Albert won't leave [her] alone" (line 163). Although the differences between Eliot's poem and *A Farewell to Arms* are great, Hemingway's allusion to the motif in *The Waste Land* and the Renaissance plays enlarges the scope of that motif even as the sexual roles are reversed, with the woman, Catherine, wanting to play love, not chess. In the hospital, Catherine had once also been the initiator of an invitation to love play (116), but Frederic too uses the term *play* when he in turn wishes to initiate it (309).

As if to remind us of the motif, Frederic is twice aware of card games going on in the café where he eats while Catherine is in desperate childbirth (318, 329). Yet the motif is also hidden in places throughout the novel, wherever the legitimacy and dedication of their love is questioned. Is it false love (mere lust or infatuation), or is it true love? One of Helen Ferguson's roles in the novel is to challenge Frederic in behalf of her friend Catherine. She doesn't believe he is serious in his courtship, and of course initially she is right. Even after Frederic and

Catherine reach the point when "I loved her very much and she loved me," Ferguson accurately predicts, "You'll never get married" and warns him not to get Catherine "in trouble" (and he does). She also observes, in emphasis of the motif of craziness, that the concussion Frederic had received "could make you crazy" (108–9). Fergy's fear is realized when Catherine becomes pregnant, and she blows up at Frederic when he surprises them on their holiday in Stresa, accusing him of not playing fairly, of using sneaky "tricks" in the game of love. Although she later apologizes for her emotional outburst of condemnation, her moral stance is justified and affirms that Frederic and Catherine are playing the game of love by their romantic rules and not by Fergy's conventional moral rules (246–49).

One other brief exchange also affirms the awareness Frederic has of playing outside conventional rules. As he later does in Switzerland, Frederic in Stresa deceives others, even an old acquaintance, the barman, about his relationship with Catherine. He asks the barman if he has seen Fergy and Catherine. "One of them is my wife," he lies, and the barman, intuiting the falsehood, jokes, "The other is my wife" (245). To Frederic the reply is not funny, and throughout the concluding book 5 he and Catherine refer to each other as if they are husband and wife. The point is not simply that the deceit is a convenience when checking into a hotel or hospital; they *feel* married to each other, even though their discussion of the actual marriage they plan after the baby is born reveals their continuing awareness of the falsehood (293–94). Their life together is neither false nor true in the context of the conventional world, where their hosts, the Guttingens, provide a paradigm of happy marriage and "true" love and where whoring and other carnal behaviors point to the opposite extreme of "false" love. In an important way their love is a synthesis of the conventional love that Fergy would have them achieve and the equally conventional love of the flesh in the Villa Rossa. In their remarkably honest, open, freely given love, Frederic and Catherine have opted out of both games.

7.

The War of the Words

If falsity in all its permutations is a principal theme of *A Farewell to Arms*, perhaps its finest and most central use is in the very language by which the false and the true are revealed. In this tension between opposites, we are dealing with the essential material of literature: words. As painting has pigments, as music has notes or sounds, as ballet has movements, literature has words. Literature also has, however, the difficulty that its materials extend into all of human life and are not limited to aesthetic uses. Indeed, our languages are discrete, complex, and ever changing, and they partly define us biologically. In this defining of our humanity, we enter a world of semantic complexity that is both the advantage of literature compared with other arts and also its difficulty.

Consider Louis Armstrong's famous Zen-like response to a request to define jazz: "If you got to ask what it is, you'll never know."[16] That reply suggests an immediacy and directness of response to music, and indeed the criticism of the fine arts may tend more to description and be considerably less extensive than the criticism of literature. That this imbalance should be so does not suggest that literature is more difficult or meaningful than the other arts. The reason for the imbalance lies largely in the difference of *materials,* and those of literature are those pesky words. Pigments and tones can be fairly precisely defined; words cannot. Further consider how commonplace are expressions of the misunderstandings of words: "I didn't mean . . ."; "You misunderstood me"; "What are you saying?" And in the vernacular equally commonplace are those expressions which reveal the delight we frequently feel when we *do* understand each other: "Gotcha!"; "You bet!"; "Precisely!" (One once-popular song touched on the problem as it pertained to the game of love: "You don't mean what you're saying / It's just a game you're playing." And in another once-popular Johnny Mercer song the lover flat-out said, "You're just too marvelous for words.") Another notorious idiom is the "you know" that peppers discussions and probably means something like "I hope you know because I don't, and I can't express myself very well."

Frederic and Catherine nicely illustrate the problem in the episode in which she tells him she is pregnant. Not by her words but by her behavior (body *language?*) Frederic perceives something is wrong, and four times Catherine denies him, insisting nothing is wrong. Finally, on Frederic's insistence she tells him she is pregnant. Ironically, she also tells him, "Everybody has babies. It's a natural thing" (138). That casual-causal statement, if she believed it, would obviate Catherine's nervousness and worry. Yet it is she who repeatedly tells Frederic not to worry, and she "reads" his response (body language again?) as a denial of his words that say he is not worried except for her. And why should he say otherwise, since he is to go back to the war and leave her alone, pregnant and unwed in a foreign country whose *language* she cannot understand? If her pending problems were not so real, the humor of the scene would be more evident.

We also know that reproduction is a commonplace of all life, and it goes on about us in the plant and animal world without requiring language. Catherine is only half-right, however, when she says her pregnancy is natural, for human beings have surrounded all essential life functions with social, political, economic, and religious languages, the words, for instance, that predictably determine Fergy's outburst because she knows "the world" makes conditions, sets rules, calls for games (no matter how arbitrary) in which words like *pregnant* and *unwed* are powerful.

Their discussion continues, with Catherine ordering Frederic to stop worrying and twice denying his judgment that she is wonderful, thus further indicating the inability of their words to connect them satisfactorily. Then "We were quiet awhile and did not talk" and "did not touch" and "were apart" like self-conscious people until Catherine reaches out and touches him and reinitiates conversation (138). But the same difficulty of communication continues, as first Catherine says something that Frederic misinterprets and then he says something that she takes offense to. It is a crucial passage in identifying this central theme of how language too is caught in the false-real trap of life, even more tellingly present because language fails even between the two persons who most passionately want to avoid its problems. The irony is implicit in the episode as it is throughout the novel.

Catherine asks Frederic, "You aren't angry . . . [a]nd you don't feel trapped?" For Frederic, becoming increasingly aware of the pitfalls of life, his answer to her second question—"Maybe a little. But not by you"—would seem to be intended, first, to be truthful and, second, to avoid giving her the idea that he thinks she has succeeded in trapping him through one of the clichéd means of female wile, deliberately getting pregnant in order to force an "honorable" marriage. Frederic *intends* to deny that he so thinks that in any way, but he has misunderstood Catherine, who promptly corrects him: "I didn't mean by me." She is not so common as to think in those love-game terms, and she is offended that Frederic would even need to deny the possibility. "You mustn't be stupid. I meant trapped at all," she says.

From one miscommunication they move to another when Frederic, presumably truthfully, replies, "You always feel trapped biologically." Just as a moment before their misunderstandings had emotionally distanced them, this answer again sends Catherine "away a long way," and she reveals what bothered her: " 'Always' isn't a pretty word." Frederic's apology does not allay her grief, but she explains her situation to him—having a baby, being in love, accommodating Frederic in every way, and then having him remind her of the biological trap of life, out of which none of us will emerge alive. Her point is not to deny the truth of biology but to *feel* rather than think, to *hope* that Frederic, her ironic, alienated lover, can move beyond his denial of life and instead affirm life, not death, praise creation and re-creation and (here) procreation. Catherine does not take amiss Frederic's acknowledgment of the biological trap. One would be foolish to deny it, and indeed an edge of joy can be found in life lived in constant recognition of transcience, making us savor life, making us avoid "killing time." It is the word *always* that reveals to Catherine Frederic's failure to recognize their opportunity to celebrate life. His timing is bad, and his flippant offer—"I could cut off my tongue"—breaks the spell just as it suggests what the snake in the garden is: false language (139).

Very often in his narrative when Frederic is confronted, he finds relief in such sardonic remarks, and here Catherine responds instantly. The distance between them vanishes as she says, "[W]e mustn't misunderstand on purpose," in the way that even lovers may perversely do, self-destroying their love. That is, Catherine knows that his offer to cut off his tongue would indeed solve the problem of misunderstanding through spoken words, but the self-inflicted punishment would not, as yet, fit the crime. Catherine's saying "You mustn't mind me" must be out of character, must be her momentary submission to acceptance of the sexist cliché of the lesser intellect of women, but it is a gambit too, a way to bring them back together emotionally, and she continues to control. When Frederic changes his prior accolade, "You're pretty wonderful," to "[Y]ou're too brave," Catherine challenges him: Who *said,* she insists, "The coward dies a thousand deaths, the brave but one"? (140). She recognizes that the ways by which we reach false positions and assumptions are through language. If the snake in the Garden of Eden brought evil and death, it brought them through its forked tongue, the very symbol of lying in Native American sign language. In Eden occurred the happy fall because our tongueless, innocent lives were given speech, at once our glory and our doom, as John Milton recognized in calling it the happy fall.

This tense scene continues with yet another challenge to words when Catherine exchanges pontifications about the brave, and Frederic (acerbically? at least ironically?) says, "You're an authority"; here Catherine recognizes he has scored a point in this language game, as she concedes his admonition was deserved. The episode may at first seem to be casual, merely an advancement of the plot to introduce the important pregnancy. But even more important is the advancement of the theme concerning words, how language, or our intended communication, fails. Catherine, however, does salvage a clever and "true" meaning when Frederic corrects her overevaluation of a .230 hitter; he is "still a hitter," still an active player in the game of life.

Their lovers' quarrel having turned to the topic of bravery then ends there, as they both make conciliatory, parallel statements: "We're both brave" (Frederic) and "We're splendid together" (Catherine). But characteristically distinguishing them is the sincerity of Catherine's exaggeration, *splendid,* and the irony of Frederic's undercutting his *brave:* "And I'm very brave when I've had a drink." At Catherine's urging, he then drinks off a third of a glass of cognac and pours himself another drink, rather graphically illustrating his point as their conversation turns from the serious topic of resolving Catherine's fate to the humorous one of speculating on the adult future of the baby (140–41). The humor is sardonic, giving its users relief but being essentially pessimistic. The trail of their conversation defines the repeated difficulty of human relations because of the failure of language. As a tool, language is inadequate to the complex tasks of communication. As users of it, we are inadequate masters of its volatile, chimerical nature. Catherine was upset, taut, and afraid as their conversation began. Clearly, at some point she will have to tell Frederic of her pregnancy. She resists; he insists. She tells, and they drift back and forth between speech and silence, sometimes misunderstanding each other, sometimes misleading each other, approaching a fight neither wants, and a fight not about their desires or plans but about how they use words. Frederic brought them back from the brink of alienation by his absurd offer to cut off his tongue, but indeed our tongues are to be blamed when they trick and trap us, just as they are to be praised when they certify those virtues which human beings are capable of only through language (136–41).

The Private War

The theme of real and false uses of language is elsewhere present in those episodes concerning Frederic and Catherine's private life. In writing about Frederic's character, I have already noted the many instances in which he lies to or misleads others. Lying, of course, is deliberate "misuse" of language if the standard of judgment is honesty and truth. But Frederic is a pragmatist, not an idealist. His standard of judgment is success in achieving some practical or desired end, whether control of his ambulance unit or seduction of Catherine.

Early on we are alerted to the importance to the narrator of the precise use of language, as in the vivid description in chapter 1. Further, we learn that he is bilingual in Italian and English (22). Later we learn that his use of French was good enough to make one Italian officer think he was French (60), and frequently in the course of the story he notes little confusions of speech, as when Rinaldi is struggling with English and takes literally what Helen Ferguson means only rhetorically (20–21). Frederic is quite aware of the power of language, and in one scene with the Italian-American officer we learn that Ettore's power derives directly from his fluency in two languages. He speaks idiomatic English (for instance, "So long. Don't take any bad nickels"), and he disparages the American opera singer Ralph Simmons because "He can't pronounce Italian." Similarly, Ettore's fluent Italian gives him an edge on Frederic in getting promoted. Frederic doesn't "know the Italian language well enough . . . to be a captain" (120–23).

Language is power when Frederic does know Italian well enough to mistranslate for ignorant Catherine the barman's warning about drowning to "Good luck" (269), and in his first meetings with Catherine, they are aware of the *way* in which they communicate. In their very first conversation, they have a hostile exchange that Catherine redirects by asking him, "*Do* we have to go on and talk this way?" (18). At their next meeting, he picks up on an idea suggested earlier by Catherine's head nurse. *We* and *they* are identified by our languages, and the British head nurse asks Frederic why he didn't join up with *us*, his fellow English-speakers, and not the Italians, who, despite their "beautiful language" are not "us" and not welcome as visitors at her hospital (22–23). When that evening Catherine rebuffs Frederic's advances, he regroups by using the idea of the head nurse, who chauvinistically derogated the Italians and accepted Frederic simply on the basis of their common language. As noted before, his "line" invites Catherine's pity merely because his work precludes speaking English—his mother tongue. The appeal is "nonsense" to Catherine, but it works and she yields to his kiss (26–27).

At several points Frederic thinks similarly of the Italians, with their theatrical helmets and ways of saluting, and the regulation requiring him to wear a ridiculously designed pistol gives him "a vague sort of shame when I met English-speaking people"—that is, the British and other Americans, who presumably are united in their ethnicity and language and contrast to the theatrical Italians. Frederic reinforces this motif here by noting that the English gas mask he carried was "a real mask"—a wonderful oxymoron beyond its literal meaning (28–29). For a character who often dissembles, this little joke is revealing.

After Catherine extracts a lying admission of love from Frederic, she then drops the game and gently admonishes him: "Please let's not lie *when we don't have to*" (31; my emphasis). And she reveals her own careful ear for language when she tells him that he pronounces "Catherine" differently from the way her dead fiancé did. Frederic is after all not, as revealed by language, the surrogate of her beloved. And when do they "have to" lie? They do not begin lying *together* until after his wounding, when he finds himself truly in love with Catherine and they begin "making" love. On the eve of his operation, Catherine counsels him, if not to lie, at least to conceal the truth of their love when, under anesthesia, he may "get very blabby." But Frederic says that he won't talk, and Catherine admonishes him for bragging, which is a kind of lying.

Their talk then shifts to a humorous inquiry by Catherine of Frederic's prior lovemaking experience. When he denies having any, Catherine says:

"You're lying to me."

"Yes."

"It's all right. Keep right on lying to me. That's what I want you to do." (103–5)

And that is what he does in this comic scene, except when Catherine signals that she really wants to know the truth in answer to one question: Does a prostitute and her client say they love each other? Frederic tells the truth: yes, if they want to. But then, unknown to Catherine, he lies and says that *he* never told another woman he loved her. Catherine is deceived, and the lie elicits her profession of love for him. But what is the moral impact of the lie? Is it one of those which Catherine had earlier acknowledged as a "white," or forgivable, even necessary, lie? And how is one to understand the narrator's (Frederic's, of course) curious interruption of their dialogue with a sentence of description of the sunrise *outside* his room and a sentence that echoes Catherine's earlier observation that her bathing him and giving him an enema in preparation for his operation had made him "clean inside and outside"? Cleanliness of mind is also at issue, and Frederic's successful lie belies Catherine's love that she then avows, now convinced that Frederic is sincere. In their first lovemaking she had repeatedly asked for confirmation of his love (92–93). Now his white lie convinces her. She has cleaned his body inside and outside, and she is finally very happy.

The irony of this scene is echoed elsewhere throughout the novel, and it is to Catherine and her fierce desire to protect the all-important word *love* from corruption that Frederic owed his growing awareness of how language and its use and misuse are at the heart of our joys and sorrows, our knowings and unknowings. When they first make love, Frederic tells Catherine, "Don't talk" (92), and when they later talk about the upcoming operation, he brags he "won't talk a word" (104). Between those opposite illustrations lies the whole of the language theme. In the first case, actions will speak louder than words, Frederic's order says, and Catherine's question after they have *made* love (not spoken of it) confirms her agreement: "Now do you believe I love you?" (92). In the second case, the passage confirms their agreement that words nonetheless have power. We may survive the sticks and stones of life (to a point), but names *will* hurt us, just as misused words will. The word *love* has power, and Frederic with seduction on his mind will misuse it. Catherine will retrieve and refurbish it and make sure they use it well, including trying to keep it their secret. Frederic will acknowledge its power when, after their first lovemaking, Catherine asks for confirmation of his love: "Don't *say* that again," he says. "You don't know what that does to me" (93; my emphasis).

Chapters 25–26 link the motif of talking with that of thinking. The former language activity is open; the latter, closed within the head of the thinkers. Throughout Hemingway's other work (as well as throughout *A Farewell to Arms*), nonthinking is a valid, even valuable state. It is not stupidity or the opposite of thinking, but it is a way of coping with irrational and absurd reality.[17] These pivotal chapters present Frederic as a changed man, physically changed by his wounding, emotionally changed by his love of Catherine. The war has also changed to the worse, and the mood of Frederic's fellow soldiers is bleak and low but often gentle. Frederic's summer of love in Milan was a "terrible" summer at the front—a word used by both Rinaldi and the priest (167, 168, and 177). Frederic's and Rinaldi's response to the depression of the former's separation from Catherine and to the latter's immersion as a surgeon in the carnage of battle wounds is the same: don't think. "I was going to try not to think about Catherine," Frederic thinks, and Rinaldi, having thought about the terror of the war, claims, "I never think" (166–67). Rinaldi then proposes the anodynes of drink and sex to share with Frederic in the night, just as they will share the anodyne of unreflective work in the day. But recovering from jaundice, Frederic cannot get drunk, and he will remain faithful to Catherine.

Just as with words, so with thoughts. They are used and abused. Even though Rinaldi and Frederic do not wish to think, they do. Twice Rinaldi immediately contradicts his pose of nonthinking—he characterizes himself as the snake of reason, and he admits he is "tired from thinking so much" (170–71)—and his subsequent drunkenness leads merely to wild fluctuations of mood. He departs by saying to Frederic, "You want to talk to the priest," an observation suggesting Rinaldi's understanding that his futile actions of trying to revive their old drinking and whoring (the latter may have given Rinaldi syphilis) must give way to that which the priest, Frederic's other friend, may give him (175).

The priest's first question indicates his awareness of how words are used: "Well, . . . how are you really?"—the "really" converting the superficial, conventional query to one of essences (177). The words the priest wishes to hear are true words, not the false ones of much human intercourse. In this short chapter of four pages of their conversation, they repeat a few words often: *think* (and *don't think*), *feel, realize, talk* and *say, know* (and *not know*), *believe* (and *don't believe*), *hope, don't mean,* and *wisdom* (and *wise*). It is a minidrama in epistemology applied to their understanding of the war. Although these friends are both war-weary, they do not think similarly about the outcome of the war. Nonetheless, back and forth they *talk* about it, exchanging their thoughts and hopes; the main effect, though, is that Frederic's pessimism discourages the priest. (He twice says, "You discourage me.") And their bleak talk leads Frederic to say, "Now I am depressed myself," and to describe how his talking articulates the thought he had tried consciously to suppress but had "found out in my mind without thinking" (178–79). Such deep thoughts originate beneath the usual superficial mental processes; they originate from an alert living, from receptivity to experience with one's senses keen, one's mouth shut.

The chapter is a remarkable tour de force, the effects of which are subtly presented in the seemingly casual and realistic narrative. In addition to the repeated words just noted, there are more than 30 negatives (*no, not, nothing, never*) and no affirmatives, and other repeated words like *beaten* and *defeat* are affirmed while repeated words like *victory* and *won* are denied. Neither Frederic nor the priest believes "in victory any more," and although they both allude to Christianity, the exhausted Frederic brings their pessimistic conversation to a close by sardonically answering the priest's question "What do you believe in?" with "In sleep" (179).

How do we know? How can we understand? The two friends here make the most pointed presentation in the novel of the futility of the human mind to comprehend the stupidity and absurdity of human action. The brief episode is full of contradictions, paradoxes, and ironies that are elsewhere dramatized in the novel. On the one hand, the priest, with his faith, is "surer of himself now than when" Frederic had last seen him; on the other hand, Frederic's talk is persistently erosive of the priest's hopes. Frederic observes that the beaten peasant has wisdom but that if given power he would be as stupid and ineffectual as all other leaders. Frederic also turns conventional wisdom on its ear with the oxymoron that victory may be worse than defeat and that defeat may be better than victory. In a sense, Frederic's grimly playful words were predictive, for a month after the novel's publication (September 1929), the stockmarket crash signaled the beginning of the Great Depression for the victorious United States and its allies, whereas the rise of Hitler in defeated Germany (1933) brought that nation relative prosperity for a decade.

The episode ends with the pessimistic and travel-exhausted, still-recuperating Frederic affirming belief in sleep, in the truth of the body if not the mind. The courteous priest apologizes, and Frederic responds politely. Indeed the turnaround here is comically instructive. The two friends get nowhere in their thinking and in their resistance to thinking. But in their *being*, in their kind behavior toward each other, in their demonstration that no matter how futile and pessimistic their thinking and nonthinking are, they can absurdly yet sincerely tell each other "I like so to talk with you" (the priest), "It is very nice to talk again" (Frederic), "I'll see you when you come back" (the priest), and "We'll have a walk and talk together" (Frederic). That is, the acts of talking (and walking), not what is said, because our language may deceive and frustrate us, but *saying, acting, being* in this world together, forming in friendships and love union against the crazy, the false, and the void—that is the good.

The greater such union is that between Frederic and Catherine, and there too Hemingway enforces the theme of the ultimate failure of words that, paradoxically, can be seen and proved only through words. It is our human condition, tragic yet ennobling. Reading and rereading the problematic chapters 38–40, I find my own subjective responses tied to this theme.

Is not Frederic's characterization of this period, "We had a fine life. . . . And we were very happy" (306), undercut by the newspapers that remind him "Everything was going badly everywhere" (292, 308, 310–11), by his worries about the biological determinism of Catherine's narrow hips (294), by his not wanting to *think* about his friends Rinaldi and the priest (but he does) (298–99), by his insomnia "thinking about things" (301), by his not wanting to "talk about" his family, because he will then "start to worry about them" (304), and finally by his and Catherine's premonition, "a feeling as though something were hurrying us and we could not lose any time together" (311)? Repeatedly in these three chapters Frederic affirms their happiness, but repeatedly the thoughts that will not be suppressed keep telling him "Time's wingèd chariot" is "hurrying near"—as earlier he had quoted from Andrew Marvell's poem as a preface to an exceptional point in their relationship when he wants "to talk facts," as if in grudging recognition that talking may be functional. (But Catherine bamboozles him with vague answers [154–55]).

I may want to raise my eyebrows; I may want my head to tell me how self-serving, sexist, and convenient for Frederic is Hemingway's solution of the plot. But given the rest of the story, it is inevitable, and the play of the words moves me in another way into a tragic trajectory, a transcendental understanding beyond the obvious level of the realistic conclusion, for what is happening in these three chapters is both organically linked to the long last chapter and also a demonstration of yet another paradox with which the novel is rife. Their life *is* idyllic, and they are very happy, but that happiness is inevitably seen and felt by Frederic, even defined by him—through the unhappiness of the brutal war, the often-difficult abrasions of human relations, and the knowledge of our biological destinies in death. One cannot be happy and wise without also knowing our mortality. Catherine too perceives the unreal, transient nature of their idyllic life: "We live in a country where nothing makes any difference. Isn't it grand how we never see any one?" (303). Theirs is a temporary cloud cuckoo land in the home of the cuckoo clock.

And their language does double service, lying for us. Or not. In the last chapter, then, the winged chariot is a taxi that takes the falsely named "Catherine Henry" to the hospital where she will die. The day begins with kind talk between Catherine and Frederic. It also includes Catherine talking about the "fine pains" of labor. "When the pains were bad she called them good ones," Frederic notes, and his immediate response to a bartender's wishing them good luck in the birthing is "Give me another glass of wine," yet another instance of an illogical and comic but realistic response, like Frederic's then talking to a stray dog (314–15). That is how our language works in its full range of possibilities, from open, honest, comforting, "true" communication to absurd communication or none at all.

The true and the false continue in this dialogic chapter in which their doctor says, "Things are going very well," and since Catherine says, "It's wonderful," Frederic jokes, "We'll get some [anesthesia gas] for the home" (316–17). Dressed in a hospital gown, Frederic thinks he looks "like a false doctor" who then gets the news from Catherine: "I'm not going to die now, darling. I'm past where I was going to die. . . . I won't die, darling." "You will not do any such foolishness," the doctor absurdly replies, and Catherine echoes him—"It's silly to die"—as we nearly die in black laughter, the diabolic language falsely sounding in the midst of a tragic scene of mounting grief (319). Even after Catherine begins hemorrhaging, the doctor repeats his "silly" admonition (331).

As Frederic waits for the doctor to "send *word*" when he may return to Catherine (my emphasis), he again reads a newspaper and then begins an internal dialogue with himself on Catherine's fate, triggered by his looking at his watch, that awful memento mori, the great product of Switzerland, that terrible bomb ticking away in his pocket. After reading his timepiece, in the following long stream-of-consciousness paragraph the word *time* appears seven times, and four times it is preceded by *bad*. Many other words relating to chronology and temporal sequence are also in the paragraph, such as *first, always, once, now, never,* and *end*—more than a dozen in all. The emphasis on time is also stressed through Frederic's fast and repeated shifts of verb tenses, from the *present* he is so concerned with, to the *immediate past* before entering the hospital, to the *remote past* of the time of the baby's conception, to the *more remote past* before modern medicine, and to the imagined *future.* Midway through the paragraph, he asks himself the dreaded question "And what if she should die?" The self-admission of contingency and uncertainty is then repeated nine times, once for each month of Catherine's pregnancy, and the refrain becomes insistent at the end of the paragraph, where in half of the last 10 sentences Frederic asks himself five times, "What if she should die?" (320–21).

The tour de force of the remarkable paragraph is a campaign in the war of the words fought within Frederic's head as he argues with himself, alternately feeling guilt and entrapment: "And this was the price you paid for sleeping together. This was the end of the trap. . . . You never got away with anything"; next rebutting himself, "Get away hell! . . . Don't be a fool"; and then reassuring himself, "She's just having a bad time. . . . It's just nature giving her hell."

The sequence is interrupted by the doctor, who somewhat indirectly answers Frederic's concerned question about Catherine. Having just demonstrated in his own interior monologue that his language cannot serve him, cannot help him understand, Frederic must then ask the doctor, "What do you mean?" Throughout this conclusion the men and women of science—persons one might expect or at least hope to be precise and accurate in language as well as with the scalpel and thermometer—are no more able to speak truly than anyone else. Indeed, medical professionals tend to deny what their experience and senses reveal. In answer to Frederic's asking whether the stillborn baby is all right, the doctor says, "He's magnificent. He'll weigh five kilos." With points of view radically different from Frederic's, two nurses joyfully enter the gallery of the surgery, insensitive to and ignorant of their effect on Frederic. Another nurse, knowing who he is, orders him into the surgery against his will, ignorant of his fear. Frederic refuses to accept the clichés and lies of fatherhood, thinking of the baby as looking "like a freshly skinned rabbit" and rejecting the clichéd remarks of a nurse: he is *not* proud of his son; he did *not* want a boy.

The false-real theme is continued visually with the disguise motif, as Catherine's face is covered with the anesthesia mask and the doctors and nurses in surgery are masked, suggesting to Frederic not a lifesaving science but "a drawing of the Inquisition" (324–25). And indeed Catherine had told him in the language of torture that her bravery was gone and "all to pieces. . . . They've broken me" (322–23). But absurdly, to the surgeon and her nurse, postoperative Catherine, exhausted and in dreadful pain, is "all right" (325–28); similarly, Frederic, in ignorance, says of the dead baby, "He's fine" (326). In this conventional but essentially absurd language, Catherine's nurse repeatedly admonishes her not to *talk,* and Frederic too once picks up the refrain and then himself is signed by the nurse putting "her finger to her lips" (326, 328).

Indeed, the story ends with the failure of language and in silence. As at other times of crisis, Frederic "was not thinking" and "tried not to think" (329). The enormity of life in the midst of death seems to deny the use of thought and speech. Yet as Catherine's death looms and Frederic "did not think, . . . could not think," he, the man who has just acknowledged he "had no religion" (327), silently *prays,* now invoking God to intercede. But just as he had recollected his own failure at being a messiah for the ants in his campfire, so God fails to save Catherine (328). Brave Catherine acknowledges in words that she is "going to die," but Frederic cannot acknowledge that and joins the nurse and doctor in denying the truth: "You're all right." Before that, in his prayer, he had acknowledged that God's "taking" the baby was "all right," and *four* more times he insists to Catherine that she is "all right," insisting on what is not true, affirming the false.

Catherine then joins in this last act of the failure of words. She had wanted to write Frederic a letter for this fatal contingency but had not done so, and twice after the doctor admonishes her for *talking* too much and for *thinking* she was dying, she joins in the refrain: "All right." Three times the doctor admonishes Catherine and Frederic for talking too much; Frederic observes that "It was very hard for her to *talk*"; and as he leaves the hospital room at the doctor's request, he says, "I'll be *right* outside" (330–31; my emphasis).

But nothing is right, and talk is wrong. Catherine's last words to Frederic are "It's just a dirty trick," echoing Frederic's own concept of the dirty *trap* of life. Negation of the truth through language completes the story. The doctor says, "There is nothing to do," and then, more pertinently, "[T]here is *nothing* to *say. I cannot tell* you—" and Frederic interrupts him to agree: "There's *nothing* to *say.*" Nor does Frederic wish to hear any more of the doctor's bedside manner, and he again cuts him off: "I do *not* want to *talk* about it" (331–32; my emphasis). There are three *nothing*'s, five *no*'s, and six *not*'s in the last 22 lines, and *saying, telling,* and *talking* have succumbed with Catherine in the war of the words.

That is where the *story* (something that is told) really begins, however, for as Frederic walks *away* in grief and in defeat, acknowledging the failure of language—"It was like *saying* good-by to a statue"— he walks *to* the story (332; my emphasis). He will resurrect the vitality of language; he will empower words once more, now in the knowledge of how we mean and demean them. He will become the writer, the teller.

The Public War

In the early encounters between Frederic and Catherine the war of words is fought between them in his private attempt to seduce her, and so too is the war fought publicly elsewhere, and nowhere more clearly than in the justly famous episode midway through the novel (in chapter 28) wherein Frederic directly addresses the problem of false language. But even before those direct reflections on the corruption of language, time and again Frederic presents himself as a person attuned to language and its uses and abuses. As noted before, he is something of a linguist, with knowledge of Italian, French, and German as well as English. He also recognizes his linguistic limitations. He is not fluent in Italian, and his fellow officers sometimes use English or pidgin Italian to be clear to him, just as he sometimes translates for their benefit (for instance, 7–8, 14, 20, 22–23, 35).

In the drunken revelry of the officers' mess, Frederic thinks they "talked too much," and in conversation with the priest, he feigns knowledge in order to be polite but does not understand what the priest is talking about (chapter 7). Instead, he plays with the language (punning on Ireland-Island) and then enters into the exchange of jokes that play with language in Italian and thus are only half-understood by Frederic. Rinaldi at one point and Frederic at another express disbelief, and Frederic drunkenly argues with Bassi over their real names (38–40). The episode illustrates Frederic's awareness of the uncertainty of what we often mistakenly and unthinkingly assume is a means of communication. Here the theme of identity is coincidental with that of language.

Frederic's language skills are not unlimited. But they are impressive enough to give him the confidence to play a small joke on the English ambulance driver who helps him after his wounding, pretending surprise at the driver's saying he is English and not Italian. Frederic then describes the driver's Italian as "voluble and perfect," an evaluation surely calling for a degree of credulity, inasmuch as Frederic himself is not fluent. He also reveals his linguistic sophistication by understanding the driver's use of an Anglo-Indian term, *wallahs* (57–58). He attempts a bilingual pun with Rinaldo and the major, telling them the Americans would be unlikely to declare war on Turkey because it is their national bird. The Italian term for the country *Turkey* is similar, *Turchia*, but the bird is *tacchino*, a very different word, and thus "the joke translated . . . badly." Then the drunken men playfully argue both *with* and *about* words: "That is all talk. . . . I will never forget Romulus suckling the Tiber. What? Nothing? . . . [Rome is] the mother and father of nations, I said. Rome is feminine, said Rinaldi. It cannot be the father. Who is the father, then, the Holy Ghost? Don't blaspheme. I wasn't blaspheming, I was asking for information" (75–76). Here semantics and grammar are stood on their heads, in friendly discourse, but language misunderstood and misused can also be dangerous.

Frederic becomes the victim of a language joke when the Italian

The War of the Words

barber misunderstands his nationality, having heard the porter say Frederic was an Austrian, not an American, officer. In neither Italian (*Austriaco* and *Americano*) nor English are the words closely similar; however, the episode serves to illustrate how little is needed for confusion and misunderstanding. Interestingly, one result of the confusion on the frightened barber's part is to refuse communication with Frederic: "I will tell nothing. . . . I will not communicate with the enemy" (90–91).

Another episode of miscommunication similarly affects the two Italian sisters whom Frederic and his drivers *intend* to help but only frighten with their words. As later Frederic will know just enough German to recognize that a dialect is being spoken (280), so with the sisters' language (probably Friulian); he knows that he "could not understand a word," and neither can the native Italian Bartolomeo Aymo (195). The girls do understand a few words of Italian, including "the vulgar word" for sexual intercourse. And again that little knowledge is a dangerous thing, for Aymo's repeated use of the word, even in the negative, serves only to further frighten the young sisters. "I didn't mean to scare her," Aymo explains, yet that word and his and Frederic's squeezing and patting their legs—"in a friendly way," Frederic insensitively thinks—are clear enough to the frightened sisters (196). When Frederic finally sends them off to join the retreating column of civilians, they still do not understand him, but perhaps the gift of money he gives them "talks": "They did not understand but they held the money tightly and started down the road" (206).

Repeatedly, Frederic notes problems of meaning as affected by language. He awakes from a dream that he had "in English" (198), and in another conversation with one of his drivers, even the most commonplace word, *good,* used with exactly the same reference, can be used differently and misunderstood:

> "That would be a good trip."
> "We'll have a good trip."
> [Bonello] "We'll have a hell of a trip."
> [Frederic] "That's what I mean." (188)

143

When he plays billiards with Count Greffi, the Count yields to Frederic's tongue (not English but American, Frederic carefully notes) but later asks that they switch to Italian. When Frederic does not want to *talk* about the war (direct experience), the Count switches the conversation to their reading (indirect experience), the immediacy of the war being perhaps both too painful and too incomprehensible. A truism suggests that one's own inchoate experiences are less comprehensible than those of other persons or even fictional characters. Again, a misunderstanding depends on language, here on the idiomatic difference between English and Italian. Greffi mentions a book about the war that both of them have read, but the Count gets the title slightly wrong—*Mr. Britling Sees through It*, he says, whereas the actual title of H. G. Wells's novel reverses the last two words. Frederic knows the difference between "seeing it through" (enduring something difficult or onerous, like war) and "seeing through it" (understanding the true meaning of something that is being dissembled or misrepresented, like the war). But Italian has no comparable idiom to "see through," to go beyond the surface appearance of things to essences. Frederic does not explain the little linguistic error that represents the great problem of truly understanding, but he further and rather perversely confounds the gentle Count by another linguistic point, twisting his use of *soul* from the general meaning of "essence" or "central, integral quality" to its theological meaning and denying that he knows about the soul (259–63).

In the rest of their conversation, they semantically fence over the meanings of words: *soul, wisdom, cynicism, religious devotion, love,* and a word Frederic uses and instantly regrets: *death.* After all, the Count is 94 years old, "But he did not mind the word." Appropriately for this theme of language, it is the *word,* the mere representation of something, that has power, not the condition of life or death itself. Similarly, Catherine had needed the word *love* to be spoken by Frederic; the sisters had been frightened by the word for sexual intercourse, and the barber by the word for Austrian; and at the Caporetto disaster, "The word Germans was something to be frightened of." At this point, an attentive survey of the words in this passage reveals that understanding of the truth is hard to come by. In the midst of the fog of battle, Frederic includes these words to describe his apprehensions and his seeking clarity and the truth: "We heard that. . . . we heard that. . . . In the night word came . . . The captain . . . told me. . . . He had it [that is, received word] . . . and said it was a lie . . . received orders. . . . I asked. . . . he had heard. . . . The word Germans. . . . 'they say. . . . They say. . . .' 'Where do they hear this?' . . . 'The word that . . . came from. . . .' 'you tell me. . . . But get the orders straight. . . .' 'The orders are. . . .' 'Tell me. . . .' " And finally, after this inquisition and demonstration of the importance and problematic nature of words, Frederic is satisfied: "All right"—not that all *is* right but simply that under the circumstances Frederic has done what he could to approach if not know the truth and is now willing and able to act (186–87).

Language—words—betray Frederic at the turning point of the retreat. First, his last driver, Piani, calls him by his rank, *tenente,* and one of the mass of retreating soldiers, illy led by their officers and resenting their power, asks who is the lieutenant and shouts, "Down with the officers!" That is what Frederic is, all right, but the solution to the threat, triggered by a "mere" word, is for Piani to call him not *tenente* but by his neutral name (219). Piani, however, is controlled by force of habit and the power of words; after a time in which Piani never calls Frederic by his name (although Frederic once uses Piani's first name, Luigi), he twice reverts to calling him *tenente.*

Words betray Frederic when the *carabinieri,* the battle police, pull him from the mass of retreating soldiers. He resists their arrest and is further frustrated in that they do not answer his repeated questions: "He did not answer. . . . They did not answer. They did not have to answer. They were battle police." The passage is a fine illustration of how one privilege of power is silence. And the victim is condemned by his very speech, as one of the arresting officers says Frederic "speaks Italian with an accent" and they can thus conclude he is a German agitator in Italian uniform and summarily execute him as a spy. Just as the biblical Gileadites separated friend from foe with a password that the foe could not pronounce (the *sh-* of the word *shibboleth*), just as the British identify their upper class by certain language usages ("U" and "non-U" speech), and just as we stereotype and ridicule one another by imitating real or imagined speech habits of ethnic, social, or economic groups, so too is Frederic the victim of his own tongue. Overhearing the summary courts-martial of the two officers ahead of him, "trials" to which the brave lieutenant colonel responds that "The questioning is stupid," Frederic sees how language is being abused. What is said has a tenuous relation to reality: "I saw how their minds worked; if they had minds and if they worked" (219–25). The good soldier Frederic, dutiful and loyal despite a growing skepticism, going so far as to himself deal summarily with the two sergeants who disobeyed his word, is driven to the brink of execution before he makes his "separate peace" (243). Later, en route to Milan and Catherine, he thinks again of the absurdity of a shibboleth and makes for himself a little joke of explanation and justification: "If they shot floorwalkers after a fire in the department store because they spoke with an accent they had always had, then certainly the floorwalkers would not be expected to return when the store opened again for business" (232).

Coinciding with the time of the Caporetto military debacle are Frederic's crucial perceptions about language (chapter 27). Language too can be disastrously defeated, just as it can be played with and used for both pleasure (humor) and understanding (wit). One of the Italian soldiers in his unit, Gino, he characterizes somewhat patronizingly as "a nice boy" and "a fine boy" (182, 185), and Gino's conversation with Frederic is at first marked by humor, some of it perceived by Frederic but not by the innocent Gino himself. About a particularly frightening artillery gun Gino says, "What's the use of not being wounded if they scare you to death?" That comic disjunction, blackly humorous, he follows with a pun. *Plateau* in Italian is *altipiano*, literally "high plain." It is " 'Alto piano,' Gino said, 'but no piano.' " Again one wonders if Gino perceives his own joke, for besides meaning "plain," *piano* means "flat" or "level," and Frederic has just described the Bainsizza plateau as "broken up." But *piano* in yet another sense means "softly," and the booming, shrieking guns of war are tearing up the plateau.

Then their comic conversation turns to military history and strategy, and further absurd disjunctions. Frederic humorously says:

The War of the Words

"If you tried to retreat to trap Napoleon in Italy you would find
yourself in Brindisi."
"A terrible place," said Gino. "Have you ever been there? . . ."
"I am a patriot. . . . But I cannot love Brindisi or Taranto"
[cities in southern Italy] (184).

Frederic asks Gino if he loves the Bainsizza plateau, where the
Italians are fighting the Austrians. " 'The soil is sacred,' Gino replies.
'But I wish it grew more potatoes' "—another comic non sequitur of
inadvertent humor. Hemingway then reinforces our understanding of
Frederic's language skills by having him use an Italian figure of
speech literally translated into English: The "dogfish" are diverting
food from the soldiers and selling it. The word represents *pescecane*
(literally fish-dog), the Italian word for "shark" and also in a figurative sense "war profiteer" or "black marketer." Even if readers do
not know the Italian source, "dogfish" still serves to suggest not only
Frederic's fluency but his awareness of the metaphoric basis of language and of the difference between what seems to be and what
actually is.

Having already used the word *sacred* to describe the soil of the
battlefield on the Bainsizza, Gino then tells Frederic that the summer's
fighting "cannot have been done in vain." Once again, as at other
critical points in the story, Frederic clams up rather than speak his
mind. He is after all a foreigner, and Gino is a patriot, a lover and
defender of his country, including the dogfish, and not like Frederic's
drivers, who see the "true" enemy not across the lines from them but
as their countrymen callously achieving selfish ends through the war.
Gino's innocence and naïveté are revealed first by his inferior linguistic
wit and second by his careless use of important words:

I did not say anything. I was always embarrassed by the *words*
sacred, glorious, and sacrifice and the expression in vain. We had
heard them, sometimes standing in the rain almost out of earshot, so
that only the *shouted words* came through, and had read them, on
proclamations that were slapped up by billposters over other *proclamations*, now for a long time, and I had seen nothing sacred, and

the things that were glorious had no glory and the sacrifices were like the stockyards at Chicago if nothing was done with the meat except to bury it. There were many *words* that you could not stand to hear and finally only the *names* of places had dignity. Certain *numbers* were the same way and certain *dates* and these with the *names* of the places were all you could say and have them mean anything. *Abstract words* such as glory, honor, courage, or hallow were obscene beside the *concrete names* of villages, the *numbers* of roads, the *names* of rivers, the *numbers* of regiments and the *dates*. (184–85; my emphasis)

Subsequently this episode will be echoed by the scene in which the brave lieutenant colonel is about to be executed; an accusing officer addresses him:

> "It is you and such as you that have let the *barbarians* onto the *sacred soil* of the *fatherland*."
> "I beg your pardon," said the lieutenant-colonel.
> "It is because of *treachery* such as yours that we have *lost the fruits of victory. . . .*"
> "If you are going to shoot me," the lieutenant-colonel said, "please shoot me at once without further questioning. The questioning is stupid." (223–24; my emphasis)

In the first episode the stupidity is harmless; in the second, fatal—and nearly fatal for Frederic too. Frederic's reaction at the river courts-martial has been determined and foreshadowed by his reaction to Gino's misuse of abstractions. Frederic has already understood the awful divergence between action and language and the unconscionable hypocrisy of *acting on* the corrupted words. Mere talk may be harmless, but unreasonable language may be linked to unreasonable act. Gino, the patriot, merely speaks nonsense; the battle police both speak it and act on it.

As in this novel, so in the actual trenches and battlefields of war do the soldiers on both sides have a growing awareness that their guns are pointed the wrong way. The ultimate foe is not on the other side of no-man's-land but is in the perverse human capacity to lie, to say that which is not. "We have met the enemy, and he is us" because of this sad proclivity. God had charged Adam to *name,* and for Frederic saturated with the meaningless abstract jargon of propaganda, "finally only the *names* of places had dignity."

Indeed, Frederic's personal insight became that of his generation, and Paul Fussell, one of the foremost historians of the war, perceived that the ongoing skepticism about and devaluation of anything in print and even language itself stemmed from the distortions, propaganda, and outright lies perpetrated by the print media and the war governments.[18] The enormity of the loss of faith in what is said, written, and meant is coextensive with our cultural values. Insofar as we debauch our language (shifting and changing though it always is), we likewise debauch our culture. Thus, the ominous silence of the battle police, who have the power of arms and authority ("They did not answer. They did not have to answer. They were battle police"), is balanced by the silence of powerlessness. When one has no language, no speech, no words, one has no power. Frederic has come to recognize this human dilemma, but in a sense he repudiates this key passage midway through his story. If he finally, wholeheartedly, and absolutely accepted the implications of his distrust of abstract words and his statement that only concrete names, numbers, and dates could "mean anything," his alternatives in action would be few. One of them he pursues as in effect he accepts the dilemma and the status quo. Having recognized the pervasive corruption of "truth" and the "good," he will nonetheless continue to function within the absurd world, holding himself aloof but not separate, even acting drastically according to its dictates when in that world's terms he orders the sergeants and then attempts to execute them summarily for disobeying his *word.*

Another alternative would be similar to that mocked by Jonathan Swift in his imagined land of Laputa, where "scientists," in recognition of the limitations of speech, do not use it but communicate by displaying things themselves and not the words for them. This nonsolution would be Frederic's if he then spoke and wrote only those names, numbers, and dates which had "meaning." Gorizia, the Isonzo River, the 69th regiment, 21 October 1917, Caporetto, Route N13—the "meaning" they have is limited and subjective. In fact, we recognize in extreme reticence pathological conditions, such as autism, or at least asocial behavior, inbred or acquired. Frederic's famous reflection about language and the corruption of abstract words is important. But it itself is a partial truth.

A third alternative to the disastrous defeat of language is Frederic's ultimate choice. Just as the Italians after Caporetto would regroup and rally at the Piave River and defeat the Austrians and Germans, so will Frederic rally and emerge from the depths of defeat and despair with his ultimate victory in the war of the words. That victory is an intricate weaving of language into a beautifully crafted whole. It is his story that becomes *A Farewell to Arms*. Frederic neither abjures abstractions nor limits himself to names, numbers, and dates. But at some unspecified time after the events of the story have taken place, he tells that story. He triumphs over both the corruption of language and the nihilism that would be inherent in a refusal to use the imperfect but perfectly human characteristic of language. Spinning out his tale, he unravels his care, and we hear in his voice a consistently sardonic tone as he returns himself, and as readers may return with him, to the middle kingdom, neither the paradise of ideal love nor the hell of war and similar human action fundamentally resulting from failures of language, failures to understand. With courage and style, then, Frederic tells his story.

Notes and References

1. C. Hugh Holman, *A Handbook to Literature,* 4th ed. (Indianapolis: Bobbs-Merrill, 1980), 274.

2. Quoted in Carlos Baker, *Ernest Hemingway: A Life Story* (New York: Scribner, 1969), 528.

3. *Ernest Hemingway: Selected Letters, 1917–1961,* ed. Carlos Baker (New York: Scribner, 1980), 273–74; hereafter cited in text as *Selected Letters.*

4. These and the preceding Robert Herrick phrase are quoted in Michael S. Reynolds, *Hemingway's First War* (Princeton, N.J.: Princeton University Press, 1976), 82–83.

5. Clifton Fadiman, *Nation,* 30 October 1929, 497–98.

6. Malcolm Cowley, *New York Herald Tribune,* 6 October 1929, 1, 16.

7. "A.C.," *Boston Transcript,* 19 October 1929, 2.

8. Judith Fetterley, *The Resisting Reader: A Feminist Approach to American Fiction* (Bloomington: Indiana University Press, 1978).

9. Donald Davidson, *Nashville Tennessean,* 3 November 1929, 7.

10. Wyndham Lewis, "The Dumb Ox: A Study of Ernest Hemingway," *Men without Art* (London: Cassell, 1934), 17–40.

11. For a complete list of the titles Hemingway considered, see Michael S. Reynolds, *Hemingway's First War* (Princeton, N.J.: Princeton University Press, 1976), 295–97, and Bernard Oldsey, *Hemingway's Hidden Craft* (University Park: Pennsylvania State University Press, 1979), 15–22. Oldsey reproduces the manuscript page listing Hemingway's tentative titles (15).

12. Harold Bloom, review of *Walt Whitman: The Making of the Poet,* by Paul Zweig, *New York Review of Books,* 26 April 1984, 3–7. Bloom specifically cites Hemingway as being in this tradition.

13. Allen Ginsberg, "A Supermarket in California," *Howl and Other Poems* (San Francisco: City Lights, 1956), 24.

14. Edmund Wilson, "Hemingway: Gauge of Morale," *The Wound and the Bow* (Boston: Houghton Mifflin, 1941; New York: Oxford University Press, 1965), 174–97.

15. See James Phelan, "The Concept of Voice, the Voices of Frederic Henry, and the Structure of *A Farewell to Arms*," *Hemingway: Essays of Reassessment*, ed. Frank Scafella (New York: Oxford University Press, 1991), 214–32. Although I disagree with some of Phelan's applications, his concept of voice is helpful and good.

16. Quoted in Ralph J. Gleason, *Celebrating the Duke, and Louis, Bessie, Billie, Bird, Carmen, Miles, Dizzy, and Other Heroes* (Boston: Little, Brown, 1975), 50.

17. For a careful and extended analysis of this characteristic and central theme throughout Hemingway's work, see Erik Nakjavani, "Hemingway on Nonthinking," *North Dakota Quarterly* 57 (Summer 1989): 173–98.

18. Paul Fussell, *The Great War and Modern Memory* (New York: Oxford University Press, 1975).

Selected Bibliography

Primary Works

Across the River and into the Trees. New York: Scribner, 1950.

By-line: Ernest Hemingway. Selected Articles and Dispatches of Four Decades. Edited by William White. New York: Scribner, 1967.

The Complete Short Stories of Ernest Hemingway. New York: Scribner, 1987.

The Dangerous Summer. Introduction by James Michener. New York: Scribner, 1985.

Death in the Afternoon. New York: Scribner, 1932.

88 Poems. Edited by Nicholas Gerogiannis. New York: Harcourt Brace Jovanovich, 1979.

Ernest Hemingway: Selected Letters, 1917–1961. Edited by Carlos Baker. New York: Scribner, 1981.

A Farewell to Arms. New York: Scribner, 1929.

The Fifth Column and Four Stories of the Spanish Civil War. New York: Scribner, 1972.

For Whom the Bell Tolls. New York: Scribner, 1940.

The Garden of Eden. New York: Scribner, 1986.

Green Hills of Africa. New York: Scribner, 1935.

Hemingway: The Wild Years. Edited and with an introduction by Gene Z. Hanrahan. New York: Dell Publishing, 1962.

in our time. Paris: Three Mountains Press, 1924.

In Our Time. New York: Boni and Liveright, 1925.

Islands in the Stream. New York: Scribner, 1970.

Men at War. Edited and with an introduction by Ernest Hemingway. New York: Crown Publishers, 1942.

Men without Women. New York: Scribner, 1927.

A Moveable Feast. New York: Scribner, 1964.

The Nick Adams Stories. Preface by Philip Young. New York: Scribner, 1972.

The Old Man and the Sea. New York: Scribner, 1952.

The Spanish Earth. Introduction by Jasper Wood. Cleveland: J. B. Savage, 1938.

The Sun Also Rises. New York: Scribner, 1926.

To Have and Have Not. New York: Scribner, 1937.

The Torrents of Spring. New York: Scribner, 1926.

Winner Take Nothing. New York: Scribner, 1933.

Secondary Works

Baker, Carlos. *Ernest Hemingway: A Life Story.* New York: Scribner, 1969. The standard biography by the late dean of Hemingway studies.

————, ed. *Ernest Hemingway: Critiques of Four Major Novels.* New York: Scribners, 1962. Includes five articles on *A Farewell to Arms (FTA)* and its "original conclusion."

————. *Hemingway: The Writer as Artist.* Princeton, N.J.: Princeton University Press, 1972. A comprehensive view of Hemingway's work, including a good chapter on *FTA.*

Benson, Jackson J. *Hemingway: The Writer's Art of Self-Defense.* Minneapolis: University of Minnesota Press, 1969. Careful analyses of various aspects of Hemingway's craft.

Brasch, James, D., and Joseph Sigman. *Hemingway's Library: A Composite Record.* New York: Garland, 1981. A useful tool of discovery of probable sources of and influences on Hemingway's work.

Cecchin, Giovanni, ed. *Americani sul Grappa.* Asolo, Italy: Magnifica Comunità Pedemontana dal Piave al Brenta, 1984. Letters, memoirs, and other writing (in Italian), plus many interesting photographs relating to Hemingway and other Americans who served with the Red Cross on and around Mount Grappa in northeast Italy during World War I.

————. *Hemingway: G. M. Trevelyan e il Friuli: Alle origini di Addio alle armi.* Lignano Sabbiadoro, Italy: Comune di Lignano Sabbiadoro, 1986. Excerpts in both English and Italian from works of the commander of the British Red Cross in Italy during World War I.

Donaldson, Scott. *By Force of Will.* New York: Viking, 1977. A thematically organized study of Hemingway and his work.

————, ed. *New Essays on "A Farewell to Arms."* Cambridge, England: Cambridge University Press, 1990.

Selected Bibliography

Grebstein, Sheldon N. *Hemingway's Craft*. Carbondale: Southern Illinois University Press, 1973. Good analyses of various aspects of Hemingway's style, including his revisions of *FTA*.

Hanneman, Audre. *Ernest Hemingway: A Comprehensive Bibliography*. Princeton, N.J.: Princeton University Press, 1967. This and the following supplement are indispensable research aids to 1975.

————. *Supplement to Ernest Hemingway: A Comprehensive Bibliography*. Princeton, N.J.: Princeton University Press, 1975.

The Hemingway Review. Special *FTA* issue, vol. 9, no. 1 (Fall 1989). Contains eight articles, including a description of an *FTA* exhibition in the John F. Kennedy Library (Boston) that houses the most extensive collection existent of Hemingway letters, manuscripts, and galleys.

Larson, Kelli A. *Ernest Hemingway: A Reference Guide, 1974–1989*. Boston: G. K. Hall, 1991. Useful update of Hanneman.

Lewis, Robert W. "Hemingway in Italy: Making It Up." *Journal of Modern Literature* 9 (May 1982): 209–36. Clarifies the differences between Hemingway's life and his fiction.

————, ed. *Hemingway in Italy and Other Essays*. New York: Praeger, 1990. Ten articles in whole or in part about *FTA*.

————. *Hemingway on Love*. Austin: University of Texas Press, 1965. Contains a chapter on *FTA*.

Lynn, Kenneth S. *Hemingway*. New York: Simon and Schuster, 1987. A recent biography, with sections on *FTA*.

Oldsey, Bernard S. *Hemingway's Hidden Craft*. University Park: Pennsylvania State University Press, 1979. Analyses of the writing and revising of *FTA*.

Reynolds, Michael S. *Hemingway: The Paris Years*. Oxford: Basil Blackwell, 1989. Biography covering the formative years right before *FTA*.

————. *Hemingway's First War*. Princeton, N.J.: Princeton University Press, 1976. A thorough study of the historical sources and composition of *FTA*.

————. *Hemingway's Reading, 1910–1940: An Inventory*. Princeton, N.J.: Princeton University Press, 1981. Along with Brasch and Sigman, an essential reference.

————. *The Young Hemingway*. Oxford: Basil Blackwell, 1986. The first part of a multivolume biography; covers Hemingway's youth both before and after his service in Italy during World War I.

Rovit, Earl, and Gerry Brenner. *Ernest Hemingway*, rev. ed. Boston: G. K. Hall, 1986. Includes discussion of Hemingway's "tutor" and "tyro" characters and the so-called code.

Trevelyan, George Macaulay. *Scenes from Italy's War*. London: T. C. and E. C. Jack, 1919. A history of the British Red Cross in Italy during World War I, probably used by Hemingway for background information and some details in *FTA*.

Villard, Henry Serrano, and James Nagel. *Hemingway in Love and War: The Lost Diary of Agnes von Kurowsky, Her Letters, and Correspondence of Ernest Hemingway.* Boston: Northeastern University Press, 1989. Biographical background to *FTA;* Kurowsky was one of Hemingway's nurses after his wounding in Italy during World War I.

Wylder, Delbert E. *Hemingway's Heroes.* Albuquerque: University of New Mexico Press, 1969. Good analyses of Frederic Henry and Catherine Barkley.

Young, Philip. *Ernest Hemingway: A Reconsideration.* University Park: Pennsylvania State University Press, 1966. A once-influential study, with some pertinence to *FTA*.

Index

Index

The Author

A native of western Pennsylvania, Robert W. Lewis received his B.A. from the University of Pittsburgh, served in Korea with the Third Infantry Division, and received an M.A. from Columbia University and a Ph.D. from the University of Illinois. He has taught at several universities in the United States and in Italy and Egypt as a Fulbright-Hays professor of American studies. Many of his publications, including the books *Hemingway on Love* (1965, 1973) and *Hemingway in Italy and Other Essays* (1990), have been about Hemingway's work. Lewis has served as president of the Hemingway Society and chair of the board of directors of the Ernest Hemingway Foundation. He is Chester Fritz Professor of English at the University of North Dakota, edits its *North Dakota Quarterly,* and continues to work on studies of Hemingway.